Fall and Rise, American Style

Fall and Rise, American Style

EIGHT
INTERNATIONAL WRITERS
BETWEEN GETTYSBURG AND THE GULF

Edited by Nataša Ďurovičová
with Hugh Ferrer

91ST MERIDIAN BOOKS   IOWA CITY, IOWA 2015

Design by Shari DeGraw

Library of Congress Control Number 2014952702

ISBN 978-0-9827466-4-6

91st Meridian Books is an imprint of Autumn Hill Books
published in collaboration with the University
of Iowa's International Writing Program

To contact AHB:
Autumn Hill Books
1138 East Benson Court
Bloomington, IN 47401 USA

www.autumnhillbooks.org

To contact 91st Meridian Books:
International Writing Program
100 Shambaugh House
The University of Iowa
Iowa City, IA 52242-2020 USA

iwp.uiowa.edu

91°ST
M
BOOKS

Contents

Introduction

Diplomatic exchange is notorious for its Potemkin villages. At its least egregious, the effort to disguise unhealthy appearances is a minor, and completely understandable vice of any house-proud nation; indeed, the rules of hospitality almost demand some misdirection. In one of his early novels, South Korean writer Kim Young-Ha fictionalizes a tragi-comic moment from his father's military service: an army officer moving heaven and earth to assure that U.S. President Jimmy Carter's visit to the DMZ will have a proper toilet available. Not only is it *de rigueur* to put a best foot forward and steer the attention of distinguished visitors away from shortcomings and blight, but it also can be sadly heroic. And yet what might be gained by tacking in the opposite direction, by inviting a delegation behind the façade, there to inspect unsparingly what is rent and broken?

Eight answers lie in the essays that follow.

Sponsored by the U.S. State Department's Bureau of Educational and Cultural Affairs, the 2011 exchange program, "Writers in Motion: Fall and Recovery," invited an international group of well-established writers into America's still-open wounds, stretching from the Civil War to the BP oil spill, the Civil Rights movement to Hurricane Katrina. These unresolved (and perhaps unresolvable) crises and reverberant, troubling legacies continue to shape millions of lives, especially in the mid-Atlantic and the South. For ten days the visiting writers, all of whom had written on — and in some cases lived — large-scale disaster in other contexts, were steeped not in easy solutions and clear-cut examples of American know-how, but in ongoing problems whose roots lie in a heterogeneous republic's intractably skewed perceptions of race, class, and federal (versus local) governance.

The shrewd reflections contained in this collection—a mixture of reportage and personal meditation—will take readers into those same wounds through the calm eyes of engaged, concerned guests; and in the process, this volume exposes the merits of a new model of diplomacy, one that dispatches with ostentation and suggests instead that there is a greater strength, an inspiring strength, in admitting that the U.S., like so many nations, must persevere through unyielding social tensions.

Hugh Ferrer
Associate Director
International Writing Program
University of Iowa

Preface

The essays in this book were commissioned to mark and cap a tour the IWP organized at the behest of the Bureau of Educational and Cultural Affairs at the Department of State in the spring of 2011, as the long sequence of anniversaries marking 150 years of the Civil War was getting underway. More generally, the invitation was to present in front of a group of writers the uniquely American trope, that of a crisis in which the seed of recovery — "a new birth of freedom," as Lincoln has it in the Gettysburg Address — is present. The DNA of this seed, a persistent sense of optimism and can-do spirit, has long been seen as one of the most powerful attractors of American culture and society, and is uniquely, remarkably, enduring. The tour's goal, and challenge, would be to check this trope of fall-and-rise against the observations and thoughts of overseas visitors, and invite a conversation: Is this optimism still a driving force in the daily life of (many? some?) Americans? What exactly makes for a "recovery"? For whom, defined by what, how long after the crisis has peaked? What is the fuel of this culture's forward-driving force — and what might be the costs of such energy?

Drawing up a travel route on a crisis map was in part determined by the raw practicalities of time, schedule, circumstances. The starting point was unquestionably going to be the crucible of Gettysburg, to be followed by Baltimore, with its convulsive urban history shaped by the aftermath of the Civil War and then the Second World War — a city familiar to most of our writers as the setting of David Simon's globally watched TV series *The Wire*. It was followed, in turn, by the next givens — post-Katrina New Orleans, and several stops in coastal

Louisiana affected by the Deepwater Horizon oil spill. Birmingham, too, with its Civil Rights battles and monuments, provided a skeleton of a "crisis-and-recovery" narrative. Our final stop was Washington DC, for a summary debriefing and a final presentation at American University, but also for a closing visit to the Arlington National Cemetery, where so many crises of modern American history can be counted in headstones.

The participants we invited were IWP alumni or visitors to Iowa City, that is, writers who were already somewhat familiar with the U.S., as well as with the program's goals and working style. As importantly, each had already written about large-scale, often cataclysmic, social conflicts, whether as a fiction writer or as a journalist. Their task was to observe, read, annotate, discuss, then blog with some regularity, converting eventually one of the entries into a final, extended and polished essay — that is, to sketch quickly, with the eye of a traveler, then to refine that sketch with a tool set of a researcher or a poet. Before the trip, we provided the participants with a compact set of readings (listed in the Reading List), selected to provide at least a minimal frame for the places and events on the tour schedule. A filmmaker traveling with the group made the writers' reactions as much a part of her material as the sites themselves. The blog is at http://writersinmotion.blogspot.com/; the film can be viewed at http://iwp.uiowa.edu/programs/us-study-tours.

The collection in front of you turned out refractive, kaleidoscopic, unruly. As the subject matter demands.

Nataša Ďurovičová
Editor
International Writing Program
University of Iowa

Acknowledgments

A large number of people were instrumental in preparing this tour. Thank you to Jill Staggs, Margaret Ames, Jason England, Peter Carmichael, Kent Gramm, Kathryn Rett, Charlie Duff, John Biguenet, David Simon, Greg Guirard, Paul Orr, Guy Blanchard, Marti Thomas, Pam Stearne King, Jim Braziel, Sue Kim, Kyle Dargan, Sandra Barkan, and our intrepid filmmaker Sahar Sarshar.

ADISA BAŠIĆ

Fall and Recovery in Five Easy Steps

Someone dreams of having a horse
Someone has a horse
Someone dreams of riding a horse
Someone rides a horse
Someone dreams of falling off a horse
Someone falls off a horse
Someone wakes up on falling
Someone gets up and rides again.

– *Horse and Dream,* a poem for children by Dušan Radović

1 DENIAL
The neighbors have disappeared suddenly and without a trace

One day he asked me, *Do you want to come with me to my hometown?* It was the most genuine and the gentlest declaration of love I had ever received. I knew how painful it had been for him to return to the town where, a decade earlier, he and his family barely saved their skins. Three thousand people were not as lucky. He never wanted to come back. Then again, it was his special place: there were the streets where he grew up, his school, his grandfather's back yard, where he used to meet the world when he was a baby. There was an especially green river that marked his childhood, and there was a terrace on the top of his former apartment building where he took me just to check something. *What does this hill resemble to you?* He asked excitedly and a bit ceremonially when we met on the terrace in the evening. *What do you mean, what does it resemble? Well, isn't that obvious? A whale, of course, that big hill is its back, and that little one beside it is its tail.*

Judging by his radiant face, I knew that was the right answer. It was a marvelous visit, even though everything was smaller, different and shabbier than it was in his memory and his stories.

And then we passed through a street that was completely deserted. Soon I realized that all houses in it were damaged and empty. Some were burnt down, others just thoroughly robbed, wiring and plumbing cut off, plucked... *Look, the whole street is empty. Where are all these people? What happened here?* He looked at me for a long time in amazement *What do you mean, where are they? Well, killed and driven away,* he said very tiredly. I felt my cheeks blushing in embarrassment. What nonsense. What a stupid question. As if I was a reckless tourist who accidentally found herself in an unknown country, not knowing anything about its recent history. We were hurrying to leave the town before it got dark, as if the ghosts would be waking up then, as if the town had not been spooky enough by day.

It has been years since then, and of that day I remember most the back and the tail of the imaginary whale, and that frightening silence in the street without people, windows, or life. A few years later we came back to his town: a small group of rare returnees, with the help of cousins and friends from abroad, managed to reconstruct just one of the many mosques in the town that had been destroyed. During the war the Serbs had destroyed all the mosques in the town, changing its face thoroughly. Just a piece of a wall and a half-melted metal dome remained of one, of all the others all that was left were parking lots and lawns. We came to the inauguration of the first rebuilt mosque in order to visit friends of his family, and to show respect to the couple returning to their former town. We were standing to the side so as to not disturb the believers participating in the prayer, and watched the arrival of several luxurious cars. The main Islamic religious ruler in Bosnia and Herzegovina, the Grand Mufti, arrived in one of them. Dressed in nicely designed attire he stood superciliously in front of the people and delivered a speech. He spoke insultingly of those people who were not coming back to live in their hometown in Eastern Bosnia, criticized the gathered for returning in large numbers only in times of festivities, while they continue to live in other cities and countries, in which they found shelter during the massacre. He referred to the victims, all those killed people, who were making it impossible to give up on the town. The survivors looked ahead, a bit ashamed. And then the Grand Mufti in his well-designed attire got into his luxurious car and buzzed off with great speed toward his distant and safe world.

The deserted street with the destroyed houses and with no people was still mainly empty. Some of the survivors would occasionally come to visit the site of their former, now burned-down, homes. Their Serb neighbors often pretended not to recognize them, or sometimes offered to purchase what remained of their estate. What would recovery mean in a town like this? How appropriate is it to ask people to return to a place where they suffered torture? And where are those who do not share their memories, and who each and every day pass by empty houses without wondering how it was possible for whole streets to have died? What does it mean, and what should recovery look like in towns in which everyone is accustomed to these strange landscapes, having learned not to ask themselves where the neighbors they'd known all their lives disappeared to? How come there are so many black holes of oblivion in the façades of their towns, the weird grassy plinths right in the middle of the streets, on the spots where 200-hundred-year-old pearls of Islamic architecture used to stand?

Nowadays, almost twenty years after all the carnage, banishments and mass rapes, Foča, the place I visited in the aftermath of the war, is an ethnically cleansed town. A rather reputable School of Medicine was opened here. It will be easier to enroll in it for those not quite up to the competitive pressure of the bigger cities, like Belgrade or Zagreb, easier to get an education, a diploma, a career. So that the irony will be complete, the future humanitarians, here to learn to save lives, will not know anything about the previous inhabitants of this town. An acquaintance, whose sister is completing her study of medicine in this east Bosnian town, says to me: *Foča is a nice little academic town. Kind of like Cambridge, or Oxford. My sister is about to have a baby, she has been offered a job at the Med School there. She is very, very happy.* In the town where she sees an academic idyll, the surviving victims see the killed, the banished, and the raped.

A common path to recovery is denial: all we have to do is shut our eyes and (as in books by Paulo Coelho) make a really big wish. Then all our guilt, and the guilt of our ancestors, will disappear as if in a fairy tale. In what previously were concentration camps we will again open mines and factories. We will send cleaning ladies with buckets to scrub the walls of the camps that had been the sites of murders or rapes and then to reopen those same buildings as pleasant hotels and spa resorts, in which we'll wish guests a warm welcome. Now and then we will stumble and get our noses bloodied a bit — it's not easy to go through the world eyes wide shut — but we'll soon stand up again and celebrate our recovery.

2 ANGER
A cut in a black neck

Not one but dozens of empty streets welcomed me in West Baltimore. Beautiful Victorian houses, threaded one after another like pearls in a necklace, gape empty. Almost no one lives in them; some city districts look irretrievably deserted. *Look, the whole street is empty. Where are all these people? What happened here?* I thought to myself again, this time in totally different circumstances. Charlie Duff, our charismatic and genteel guide, clarifies that there are three reasons why this is so. The first is that cars enabled people to move to peaceful suburbs; the second is the de-industrialization of Baltimore; the third is race. Freshly arrived immigrant workers who might live in these houses had stopped coming, and the small number that remained had moved away, grouping themselves in their "cleansed" black and "cleansed" white neighbor-hoods. Much more time is needed for segregation to be abolished in reality than it is in theory, and in the law books. A majority was deter-mined to live separately, so the City Councils did their best to help them: Charlie is showing us the gas station, the street and the shopping center that were built a couple decades before, as a kind of buffer zone between *white* and *black* districts. Even in the official documents this project is mentioned as a *fire break,* the cut made to prevent the spread-ing of a fire. The American racial and the Bosnian ethnic segregation shock by how similar they are.

Following Baltimore and its introductory lesson on race issues came Birmingham, Alabama. And the depressing lesson was repeated, for the human race does not learn from experience. We repeat our mis-takes with persistence and determination. After burning our fingertips on a smoldering surface, the next time around we press the whole palm against the same surface with all our strength, without flinching and without hesitation. Historic lessons are nonexistent; history as the teacher of life only exists in dusty Latin textbooks, cracked open by a few new but distracted students of a classics grammar school. Just when one Calvary is over, we hurry up another one. World War I was followed by World War II. *No more Auschwitz, No more Holocaust* was followed, in short order, by apartheid and genocides in Cambodia, Rwanda, Bosnia.

At the Civil Rights Institute in Birmingham, where an interactive exhibit depicts the history of the struggle against race discrimination in the U.S., one feels the same abashment as after the visit to The U.S. Holo-caust Memorial Museum in Washington, DC, or to The Memorial Centre in Potočari, Srebrenica. First the disbelief that someone could even think to play God, to decide the life and death of other people, to consider oneself so superior in value and dignity. Then the same insight about the banality of human evil. Then the exhibits telling the story of someone inventing the division of the most ordinary daily lives into two colors, black and white: separate urinals, classrooms, means of transportation, restaurants, barbershops, grocery stores...

Several exhibits in this memorable Birmingham museum are especially striking. The first is the snow-white uniform of a Ku Klux Klan member, with its neat (a poet fond of romanticizing can barely refrain from writing "loving") seam work. Next to it, a small explanatory tag with two words: *anonymous donation*. That means someone kept this item in the family closet, perhaps hidden and perhaps not. Someone realized that the world is after all a bit better if this white gown does not remain a home relic but is to be found where it belongs, in the Museum of Madness and Senselessness of Segregation. Someone anonymous: that is perhaps even more important. Because that means that the anonymous donor feels fear and discomfort, but also that he or she is slowly overcoming them. Recovery is perhaps just the decision that one day all the skeletons in our closets will end up in the second-hand shops of history, where they belong. Apart from the uniform, the glass showcase also contains a half-burnt wooden cross, which the FBI used as evidence in an investigation against some Klan members, and which was later handed over to the Museum. The year in which the cross was burnt is also frighteningly recent — 1997.

The second exhibit that attracts special attention is a picture of a black woman, a nurse. This part of the exhibition contains life-sized images of people of different backgrounds and professions. They illustrate how segregation permeated different levels of society, and ways in which people have found excuses and justifications for it. But the detail in the exhibit that makes it special was not supplied by a museum curator. Rather, it was clearly supplied by a visitor: the neck on the picture of the nurse is cut with a sharp object; the symbolism of slaughter is more than obvious. Someone did not like the concept of the Museum, or the idea of abolishing segregation. This *intervention* is again, most probably, the act of a reckless and spoiled teenager on a school visit, one who thought cutting the black neck would be really funny. We don't know, and can't know, for certain whether the explanation really is that banal. We don't know, and can't know, for certain whether anyone was there with the person who cut the neck of the nurse, and we don't know anything either about how that made the participant or participants feel. Were they thinking about what had happened until the end of the day? Did they tell anyone? Did they brag about their *mischief*? It is interesting, though, that the staff of the Museum did not correct or repair this act of vandalism. And that they did not offer any additional explanation for it.

The third Birmingham exhibit at which I stopped for a long while was a picture from the protests *against* the abolishment of segregation. After all the marches and protests had finally ended, after the humiliation and discrimination had finally been outlawed, groups of citizens started organized *civilized democratic* protests. One woman in the photograph attracted my special attention. She is pretty, wearing lipstick, her hair neat, dressed in a beautiful cinch-waisted dress in the 60s style. Smiling, and obviously in a good mood, as if she had just come back from a date. This attractive woman (she would have to be an old lady today, and might well still be alive) has been captured in a public protest, struggling for those absurdly separated urinals, classrooms, restaurants, barbershops, grocery stores, public transportation, for all that had been abolished after a great effort... It is hard to accept that there is a democratic right to fight for an unfounded, pathological really, idea about one person's domination over another. I imagine how that attractive woman comes home after the protest, takes off her elegant but somewhat tight shoes, lies down on a sofa and puts up her feet to have some rest. Perhaps she is welcomed by her loyal black servant, who raised her, offering her coffee and a sandwich as a refreshment, to get back her strength after the protest march.

3 DEPRESSION
Just wait for the witnesses to die

When does the process of recovery truly begin? Does it happen with the death of the last witness, the one who still remembers all too well? Traumatic experiences cut deep into one's memory with a terrifying precision. A decade after it has all been over one can still hear women in Bosnia describe how their husbands, sons, relatives were taken away to be killed: *This is how they took him away... He looked at me this way... He was wearing a tracksuit just like this one... As we were parting, he told me... I gave him... He turned back, I can still see him so vividly... That hair of his... And how he shuffles a bit as he walks... I told him "take your sweater, you'll catch a cold"... He turned toward me and smiled... I can still see him so vividly...*

As long as people who remember are alive, the recovery is painful and slow. Because only a recovery that is slow and sticks in one's craw is somewhat bearable, and just, in this unjust world.

Once the living witnesses are gone, only myths remain. Once the witnesses whose stories have never been heard die, the only thing that remains is a blank blackboard, ready to be inscribed with whatever we wish. When witnesses die, new children are born. Prospering, rosy-cheeked, happy. The children for whom the world begins with their birth. They have no sins, no obligations, no memories. Fluttering like beautiful flags raised high on their poles, they are pledges for a better tomorrow. They haven't done anything wrong. Nothing can be held against them...

And when the witnesses who saw people being crucified, hung from a tree, set on fire in locked buildings or blown up, have died, the time comes for the new, the different, the better.

Once the witnesses are dead, new children grow up to believe that the world is a magical place. Some of those children are born in countries that have, in the meantime, become quite civilized.

As witnesses die, kids grow up happy and free from responsibility. *That's our American optimism,* says a nice boy who does not know whether his grandfather was a member of the Ku Klux Klan. He does not know because that story belongs to yesterday, and it is for them to look far, far ahead. It would be impolite to ask the elders. Because yesterday does not exist, does it?

And so, if we choose amnesia, we will never find out. That is how we can pardon thousands of murderers, who remain nameless and faceless. That is how we will never have to attribute responsibility to any of those who pulled the trigger so many times it left a blister on their finger. That is how we might never find out who the skillful miner was who brought the explosives and set the wires the night a church was blown into the air. Or a mosque. We will never find out who shot a bullet into the back of a head. Who cut up sheets day and night to make blindfolds to cover a person's eyes before they were shot. It is impolite to ask a nice old lady, a grandmother or great-grandmother if she at least once made a cake or sent a bottle of home brew to a Klan meeting. We will refrain from asking a grandfather how it felt to hold the torch high in the air. High and proud, upright, like the Statue of Liberty. Or when he tightened his gun belt. Or when he put on the sinister hood. The *ušanka*.[1] The fez.[2]

What was on his mind as he slashed across somebody's throat with a knife? Or as he tightened the noose?

We will sit forever at a family dinner, under nicely framed photos of our ancestors, looking optimistically ahead. Far, far ahead...

---

1   Ušanka – a fur hat worn by the Chetniks, a Serbian ultranationalist irregular military force in World War II as well as in the Bosnian war of 1992-95.
2   Fez – a hat worn by the Bosnian Muslims in the past, worn also by the Muslim members of the Handschar Division, a notorious unit that was part of the Nazi Waffen-ss force in World War II.

4 BARGAINING
If we fix the facades, everything will be as it was

If we cannot or will not fully understand the reasons of the fall, let us at least try and get up as soon as possible. If we fix the facades and the roofs, perhaps everything will be as it was.

Every day bold headlines in Bosnian newspapers catch the eye. The international community is dissatisfied with the progress of reforms. Bosnia is on a slow track to join the European Union. Foreign officials are dissatisfied with the BiH situation, two decades after the start of the war. Citizens of Bosnia and Herzegovina did not do this or that... Slow, lame, confused in this fast world of ever faster technologies, we are not getting up quickly enough. When so many billions of dollars have been invested in the recovery. Our super-modern bionic prosthetic legs were so expensive but we still walk stiffly, like so many Frankensteins. And this is what disturbs the others so much.

The need to move on, so deeply rooted inside all of us, has been a useful tool throughout the centuries when people have had to rise up from the ashes over and over again. But what is recovery, and what is the *illusion* of recovery, its outer manifestation?

In the suburbs of New Orleans, entire neighborhoods have been reconstructed with so much detail that it is difficult to even imagine the disaster we heard about during our visit. It is quite difficult for the present-day visitor to the city to believe that the devastating effects of the flood have been almost completely removed in such a short period of time. Thousands of houses have been repaired, some are being repaired right now and more are completed every day. The tourist office of New Orleans offers a tour to visit the parts of town most affected by Katrina. Standing in front of a list of tourist attractions, an American woman says to her friends, all of whom obviously came to the city for a good time: *Visiting sites most affected by hurricane Katrina? Who wants to hear about that? As if we haven't seen enough on TV.* However, the minibus that takes the curious on the three-hour tour is full. The first part of the trip is so boring that it nearly puts us to sleep, passing as we do through neighborhoods (white-middle-class) that have been completely reconstructed. Some houses have been rebuilt from top to bottom, some just repainted, and only a few empty grassy spots make one uneasy, for houses used to stand on each one of them.

Most of these houses were built on pillars similar to those of lake dwellings. Some of them are about half a meter tall, some over two metres, making the houses look like strange castles floating in the air, or perhaps like strange long-legged birds that came down to this pleasant area for a short rest. Here, nature is being bargained with: we are hard workers who rebuilt all that was destroyed, but we also are smart, trying to prevent foreseeable disasters. We want to believe that there still is some order in the world, and some logic, and we truly hope we can prevent catastrophes, that we can prepare for them.

And yet, every day before our eyes, giant waves, earthquakes and floods wipe entire towns off the face of the Earth.

As parts of New Orleans are becoming ever poorer, the number of collapsing, abandoned and half-rebuilt houses is growing. In front of some of them people continue to live in trailers, gathering money and strength to repair their homes. Some houses look eerily empty. Many still have the visible sign placed there by the U.S. National Guard: the date when they entered the house, the unit's name, the number of bodies they found inside. The dates from the wealthier residential areas of the city show that help came ten days too late. In the poor areas, the help was over a month late. These neighborhoods are mostly empty even today; not even shops, hospitals or schools have been repaired.

Passing a trailer parked in front of a ruined house, our guide is talking angrily about the owner's *laziness,* for he did not manage to repair his house even six years after the disaster. We are very confident when it comes to assessing the time needed for a person to get back on his feet. Being slow earns, once again, our mocking laughter. We are not interested in peoples' lives but rather in the outer manifestation of their ability to fix something. We don't care if they were so scared or disappointed that they now hesitate to return to the ruins of their earlier lives, from which they were chased off by a flood or a war. The imperative is: move on, look ahead, forget about it... As if there were no situations in which people need a lot of time and courage to move on. As if there were no situations in which it is impossible to move on.

A friend of mine, an American, a poet, survived a terrible family tragedy ten years ago: he lost his four-year old daughter. After many years he wrote a book of poems about it. When I asked him if the writing had a therapeutic effect on his life, he said that the process never had anything to do with therapy, for he rejected all offers of psychological assistance. He rejected them for they begin with a premise that one can heal, that one can feel better. He said that he did not want to get over it, that even today he does not want to get over the one he loved but who no longer is here: *I want the pain to stay with me and inside of me, for it is the way for my daughter to be with me too. Therapy brings you back to a normal state of mind, and people who have experienced something very traumatic became anti-normal in a way and there is a part of them that does not want to (and I am not certain that it can) return to the normal state, that they can bury their trauma.*

This manner of understanding things is rare in the present-day world of fast repair, of belief that shards of a broken world can be (and must be) mended with a strong glue and fixed with high-quality construction materials, as if nothing had happened.

There was a great deal of compassion for and anxiety about Japan in Bosnia and Herzegovina this spring because of the catastrophic earthquake and tsunami there. With surprise, and with respect, we watched the calm faces of the people handling despair with immense discipline. In a TV interview, a woman said quietly that water had ripped her child away from her arms as she was trying to save it, in vain. The dignity that Japan had throughout the catastrophe was amazing. Seven days after the earthquake, a picture appeared on the internet, showing a highway broken up by gaping chasms, then fully repaired a week after the quake. This speed was awe-inspiring. But what about the gaps that weren't the result of natural hazards, but were created among people? Is it appropriate to ask people to return to small towns where the oppressors, whom they managed to escape, are still living—as is the case in Eastern Bosnia? Is it appropriate to ask people to take out a loan and set out to repair their home in New Orleans? Does a person have the right to not recover? Or at least the right to a slow, long-drawn-out healing process?

Do we have the right to our own ruination? The right to our destroyed house, in front of which we'll park a trailer and live in it even when all our neighbors repair their homes and start looking with suspicion upon our eyesore, standing there as witness to something they themselves wish to forget?

5 ACCEPTANCE
Life goes on, or rather...

We tend to believe that things are replaceable. Our clothes last barely a season or two, we throw away super-durable plastic dishes as soon as we are sated, our hunger satisfied. By tomorrow, everything we own will appear in a better, smaller, more perfect version. The only problem is that we are slowly beginning to believe that people can be replaced much the same way. No doubt, our job could be done equally well by many others. There are also those waiting in line to jump into our lives, to love our lovers, take our kids to day-care...

Because whatever happens, *life goes on...* There are very few things so encouraging and yet so frightening as knowing how much truth there is in this well-worn phrase. One stands up after falling down, sometimes slowly and painfully, with hesitation, other times easily and energetically, without fear. And then what? We shake off, count our losses, move on. We round off casualties to the nearest whole number. History rounds off skeletons to zero; a thousand and one is still only a thousand... When anniversaries come around we pay our respects, fix what is broken and quickly put on the mask of normalcy. We hail recovery as a sign of strength. Should a tear appear after some time, we wipe it away quickly, secretly, with a feeling of uneasiness...

One can have a pleasant time in New Orleans, remaining completely oblivious to what happened here six years ago. The city has been given a makeover for tourists, it has put on a smile, opened its shops and restaurants, offering souvenirs, massage, sightseeing tours. New Orleans again is what everyone comes for — a place of great and unlimited fun, where one can smoke in bars, listen to street music, feel free. The music festival is on, and the French Quarter is swarming with people. Old people dance vigorously in front of the stage as if faith in *flower power* never died. A group of tourists is laughing, taking shelter from the warm spring sun under a small tree: they are all wearing cheerful red lobster hats. Beautiful students dressed up in that carefully careless way move their hips to the rhythm of the music. Life triumphs. There is no yesterday. We do not look backwards.

This abundance of colours, aromas and sounds — a sunny day always makes the world look more beautiful — fights gloomy thoughts, and invites oblivion. Amnesia is healing, it makes life easier. How else could we live? On a day like this, how would it feel to think about which one of those pleasant and hospitable people, just a few years ago, was the first to take a step towards bestiality, was the first to pull a gun. And who among them was standing on the roof, with no hope of being rescued.

Blissful in our forgetfulness we taste the gumbo, throw coins to street musicians, drink cocktails called "the Hurricane" (!), and for the first time this year expose our pale bodies to the warm sun. Everything is happening *for the first time*. The power of life forces the green stalks through the cold earth of April, "the cruellest month." The explosion of this magnificent cruelty occurs right before our eyes.

All the way in the corner of the picture, a young mother of ample bosom is feeding her baby on a lawn, both unperturbed by the clamor around them. Relentless and unstoppable, life goes on... The shivers going down the spine of a bystander may just be those of excitement over the power of nature, not of bewilderment and horror.

IN PLACE OF A CONCLUSION
Wait for me and I will return...

Having examined the perennial and world-wide success of the novels of Agatha Christie, a true master of crime fiction, literary theorists have concluded (in a text I read somewhere a long time ago) that a small English village, ordered and reliable, is the perfect metaphor for the world. A crime that happens there destroys the existing balance, and it is then the detective's ability to find the perpetrator that brings back the good old world of harmony. This sense of order and harmony is like a glass of milk before bed: millions of readers all over the world crave it and never turn it down.

But all the armies of TV detectives, forensic scientists and other justice-minded men would be powerless in the real world. In reality, the investigators are not quite skillful enough, the prosecutors not incorruptible, the legal systems not all that reliable, the judges not always that strict and not even always awake (literally: take the well-known scandal of the judge Adolphus Karibi-Whyte, discovered sleeping on several occasions during a trial at the Hague Tribunal). In reality, the criminals impudently say that the witness is lying. And they say this with a straight face to dozens, hundreds of witnesses. They say to these people that they shot themselves. The war criminals stated that the two massacres that took place at the main Sarajevo market on 5th of February and 28th of August 1994, and in which over a hundred people lost their lives, were staged, with mannequins in place of corpses, even though the results of the massacre were clearly recorded by TV cameras and broadcast on many TV stations. The criminals are telling the world to its face that it is lying.

Thus, the first step on the way to recovery is to convict the criminals. It does not matter on whose side they fought; nor does it matter how fiercely, or in whose name. Until the water is back in its riverbed, until the fire is put out, until the trembling of the ground has stopped, the removal of the consequences is useless. All the peace conferences and all the rebuilt homes in the world are in vain until the world itself regains its balance. For until people regain their sense of security, and until the criminals are found and convicted, all such efforts are like houses built on shaky foundations.

In Birmingham, we visited the 16th Street Baptist Church where in 1963 four girls, Addie Mae Collins, Cynthia Wesley, Carole Robertson and Denise McNair, had been killed in a Ku Klux Klan terrorist attack. The killer, Robert Chambliss, evaded justice for a long time before he was finally convicted, fourteen years after the event. The trial is the only reliable beginning from which to start: otherwise the world loses its clear outline, making the recovery long and painful (as can be seen in Bosnia and Herzegovina). Even in historically clear situations (and there aren't many of those) there is, unfortunately, space for relativisation and for the clouding of the truth. In spite of the verdict of the International Court of Justice on the Srebrenica genocide, and even though the European Parliament declared July 11th a day of commemoration of the Srebrenica genocide (a resolution Bosnia and Herzegovina did not sign because the Bosnian Serbs blocked it), it is possible to publish books and make documentaries, mere parodies of truth, which are advertised with the slogan *"how it really happened."* It is possible to deny undeniable facts, to claim that the genocide never took place, that eight thousand people were never killed. Without the verdicts, the recovery is unquestionably harder. If our firm belief in slow but achievable justice is undermined, we'll be left with nothing except a windswept ground of different interpretations and historical phantasmagorias.

Justice must be the first step on the golden path to recovery. Not only is it slow and blind but also — experience has taught us — lame, lazy, hesitant, easily frustrated. It is capricious, hard to reach, and does things in its own way. And yet, there is nothing else to do but to fight and to wait for it — determinedly and steadily, like the girl waiting for her beloved who (to borrow from the Russian poet Konstantin Simonov) tells her: *Wait for me and I'll return/ Only wait and don't give up / Wait when you are filled with sorrow/ Wait in the sweltering heat/ Wait when the others/ have stopped waiting/ Wait even when others are tired of waiting.../ Wait for me and I will return/ Wait when they tell you to forget/ that your hopes are deceiving you/ Even when my dearest ones/ say that I am lost/ And when friends sit around the fire/ Drinking to my memory/ Wait and do not hurry to drink to my memory too/ Wait for I will return/ defying every death.*

POST-SCRIPT

At the time I first wrote this piece, Ratko Mladić, the general of the Bosnian Serb Army, was the most wanted fugitive in the world. Accused of war crimes, including the genocide in Srebrenica and the siege of Sarajevo, he remained hidden in Serbia for many years. His Bosnian victims had been waiting in vain for his arrest and thereby for the first real step toward recovery. And then, after so many years, when all hope of justice had almost disappeared, the news came of his arrest. In Sarajevo the excitement was noticeable, but there was no euphoria. The TV stations kept on running endless footage of war destruction, bringing to life difficult memories. In the news we saw once again the scenes of horror we had all witnessed. People were agitated.

This evening the atmosphere is quite unusual. The weather is warm, summer has finally decided to come, people have moved from indoor bars to street cafés. While some are toasting the occasion of his arrest, most are quiet, deep in thought. Exactly nineteen years ago, on a May night in 1992, Mladić ordered his troops to bomb the blockaded Sarajevo: "Attack them so they can't sleep, stretch their minds!" I remember those days; it was the very beginning of the siege, we were still afraid of the shelling so we'd go down to the basement every day. Our neighbor had a shelf in his basement where she kept useless old stuff. When the siege began, she turned that shelf into a secure place for her greatest treasure: it became a bunk bed in which her daughters (three and five at the time) slept. Today, these little girls are adult women, both very beautiful, with good jobs and families. One of them has recently become a mother herself.

I look at a picture of Ratko Mladić: an ordinary worn-out old man, one hand crippled from a stroke, grey hair, a sickly-pale face. I know he will spend the last of his strength trying to discredit the court in The Hague. Helpless, the self-proclaimed *God of the genocide* is no longer the god of anything. Neither has he any power left.

People in the café around me sink slowly and thoughtfully into their private memories. Somewhere behind me I hear the clink of a glass in a toast. Someone has come up with the idea of drinking to the General's good health and long life, so he can see the end of his trial and receive a fair and stiff verdict. Again I feel that life triumphs, and surprisingly that feeling does not scare me but is ultimately encouraging. No one shoots at Sarajevo anymore; the city is so quiet and still... Somehow it seems to me that tonight Sarajevo does not want to sleep at all.

VICENTE GARCIA GROYON

Theme Parks and Cemeteries: On the Fall and Recovery of American Cities

DETROIT, MICHIGAN

I set foot on American soil and realize that I have to brave the dreaded full-body scanner. I have one more flight to catch, from Detroit to Baltimore, but American air travel regulations require me to retrieve my luggage after clearing Immigration and subject it, and myself, to radiation before we can proceed.

I'm here under the auspices of the U.S. State Department and the International Writing Program to visit American cities that have undergone crises and disasters and to reflect upon the theme of "Fall and Recovery." In my initial enthusiasm, I failed to consider the amount of American air travel that this study tour would entail, and now I weigh the benefits of this commission against its disadvantages.

As I wait in line to submit myself to the indignities of the process, I observe the others ahead of me and realize that I am entering the Land of the Free through a phalanx of quasi-military trappings and procedures. While it's all too easy to snicker at the paranoia that has engendered these inutile inconveniences, they are also signals of a fearsome will to survive.

Prior to setting out on this journey, I drafted a statement of my initial thoughts on the study tour's theme, invoking the example of "once-thriving civilizations that passed out of existence." If the Transportation

Security Administration was any indication, I would have to reconsider my assumptions.

GETTYSBURG, PENNSYLVANIA

Gettysburg is a town that had its future stolen. The site of a significant three-day battle of the American Civil War in 1863, one that resulted in the largest number of casualties, it found itself suddenly responsible for the corpses of almost eight thousand soldiers and five thousand horses. The state of Pennsylvania therefore purchased several acres of farmland near the town and established a national cemetery. Before the year was over, President Abraham Lincoln delivered a two-minute speech that effectively consecrated not just the cemetery, but the entire battlefield and the town with it, binding it forever to a historic event and preventing it from becoming anything else. Today, Gettysburg is a borough that lives off its history, and is defined only by it.

Our group's experience of Gettysburg begins on the drive from Baltimore/Washington International Airport, where the writers have converged before setting out together on this study tour. As we approach the town, the houses and buildings become older and more colonial in style, although the van is moving too fast to tell if the architecture is authentic. Painted wooden signs advertising service establishments swing from poles over doorways. As we enter the town proper, the historical recreation becomes more obvious — "Ye Olde" this and that, bunting-themed décor. The town's primary industry seems to be tourism centered around the Civil War and the Battle of Gettysburg. After its consecration, the town has no other option.

A local tour company has systematized the experience. A bus ride through the battlefield with stops at significant monuments is its foundation, and one can avail of either the value plan, which adds on three historic attractions, or the full package of seven additional historic attractions, the attractions being a mix of museums and multimedia exhibits. The town is peppered with other such attractions, as well as hotels, restaurants, and shops, each one marked neatly on a map. In July, tourists can observe a live reenactment of the battle in the battlefield itself. This is tourism as Automat, a limited set of prescribed choices designed to give visitors the illusion of having experienced the town and its history.

One of the star attractions, the Gettysburg Diorama, features more than 20,000 hand-painted figures in an accurate scale model of the battlefield. A 30-minute light-and-sound show guides viewers through the battle, providing an informative geographical overview. The viewing room also includes other exhibits — historical artifacts such as weaponry, uniforms, a replica of Lincoln's death mask — that one can peruse after the show, which runs automatically upon the flip of a switch. Outside the viewing room, one passes through a gauntlet of shelves overstocked with a bewildering array of souvenir items: mugs, pins, pens, t-shirts, sweaters, refrigerator magnets, military costumes, commemorative plates, figurines, dolls, key chains, and so forth, all mass-produced outside of the U.S.

American tourism seems to be structured this way, with Disneyland as the gold standard for this model — a self-contained, fabricated series of attractions with concessions to human needs and comfort. This blueprint allows order to be introduced into the chaotic travel experience, providing the illusion of a comprehensive local immersion while ensuring several profit opportunities for the tour proprietors. Even as the fields of Gettysburg became hallowed ground, the town at its center transformed itself into a theme park, thereby guaranteeing its survival.

Our experience of the battlefield itself manages to evade the tourist trap model — our guide is Peter Carmichael, a passionate historian from Gettysburg College, who seems intent on dismantling the myths that have attached themselves to the battle and its personalities. Peter pointedly does not take us to the usual tour stops, instead leading us on tramps into the woods to stand by a brook or a shallow depression in the ground, or in the middle of an empty field. With the help of detailed battle maps showing troop positions, identified by their commanding officers and regiment numbers, and their movements at various points during the battle, he gestures here and there, indicating how the battle progressed, compelling us to imagine the scene. Then he begins telling the stories of individual soldiers who had stood, crouched, or lain where we were standing. We read from these soldiers' letters to family and loved ones, and suddenly personal narratives emerge from the monolith of history, in the words of men and women who lived through the war. Peter shrewdly juxtaposes a god's-eye view of the battle with a view from the mud, forcing a reconsideration of the grand narratives of the Civil War.

The battlefield itself is a gently rolling landscape of fields, knolls, and ridges that had once been agricultural land, edged with forests and broken by clumps of trees. The houses that stood there in 1863 still remain, either restored or rebuilt. So obsessive is the concern for accuracy here that trees are being chopped down and foliage replanted to restore the 1863 topography.

On the other hand, the fields and hills are dotted with scores of markers and monuments of various sizes, shapes, and styles, commemorating events, regiments, and individuals. Although the graveyard is concentrated in an area now called Cemetery Hill, the rest of the battlefield functions as a large memorial park.

Even as the 150th anniversary of the Civil War approaches, renewed debates about what really happened and what the war meant continue to erupt all over America. The arguments take the form of history books, scholarly articles, blog posts and tweets, or battle reenactments (some of which blatantly revise history). In Gettysburg, the nature, design, and placement of each marker and monument is subject to intense political wrangling within the Gettysburg National Military Park administration. Even when the memorial is finally erected, it might still suffer an ignominious fate if prevailing tastes and opinions compel tour guides to misinterpret or, worse, ignore it. Peter harps on the "presentation" of history in the battlefield. What is at stake is the narrative of this war, and the story or stories that will be remembered and retold.

Storytelling is a sense-making process that forces logic and meaning upon raw experience and sensation. There is a need to articulate pain, to speak it, to tell its story, as a way of making sense of inchoate tragedy. At a wake for a loved one, the bereaved are compelled to tell the story of the death to visitor after visitor in a key part of the grieving process. Abraham Lincoln set the tone for the story of Gettysburg in his two-minute speech, and since then, America has been encouraged to rise up from the blood, smoke, and dust of the Civil War by telling a story of redemption and new beginnings. Over time, through repeated tellings, the story hardens into myth, which is notoriously difficult to revise, having acquired an authoritative, definitive patina. Peter's project seems to be to slow down, even halt, the process to speckle, streak, and texture the narrative, even as other interests would rather resolve the narrative in an expeditious way so it can be left behind once and for all.

There is a sense, in the Gettysburg Address, of hastening the mourning so that the hard work of restoring peace and initiating progress in the United States can begin. The memorial therefore becomes a requisite, paradoxical, remorseful gesture to the past—both a farewell and a pledge of loyalty—that absolves the bereaved for abandoning it. Perhaps this is the only means of recovery that forward-looking American optimism can conceive of: to move on, but not to forget.

BALTIMORE, MARYLAND

Charles Duff is an impressive man—tall, patrician, imposing, he moves and speaks with the confidence of someone accustomed to being heard and followed. He introduces us to the city of his birth, Baltimore, in stages, observing a strategic progression that follows a personal theory of cities and their restoration.

On our first day, he leads us on a walk through the prettier areas of the city. We pass tree-lined avenues with narrow brick buildings reminiscent of London and old Manhattan. The occasional seagull flapping overhead reminds us that the ocean isn't far away. He points out neighborhoods organized around genteel squares, carefully restored and maintained architecture, and cultural and historical landmarks — the Basilica of the Assumption, the George Washington Monument, the Walters Art Museum, the Joseph Meyerhoff Symphony Hall. As dusk falls, we hurry in biting wind to dinner at his home, one of a block of row houses in Bolton Hill, a neighborhood where one can leave one's front door unlocked. He takes some of us to a neighborhood association meeting, where the problems of garbage can design and dog poop are threshed out in an atmosphere of civil society.

All along the way, he keeps up an incessant stream of tour guide patter, dispensing historical facts and trivia as though he was speaking of a beloved grandmother. Charlie loves Baltimore dearly, and as such sees its beauty as well as its blight, and praises and condemns it freely. Before the day is over, he has already made one of his biases clear: the automobile has destroyed the city, or at least the city model that he prefers. On our walk, he points out gaps between buildings — gaps where once stood a building, since torn down, which now lie vacant or have been converted into paid parking lots. Streets have been widened (and thus, buildings and sidewalks modified) to accommodate vehicular traffic, and the city has been allowed to expand beyond its formerly human dimensions, where everything was a walk away. Pedestrian traffic causes shops, restaurants, and other small businesses to flourish, and public services to remain in the vicinity. In a city of human dimensions, neighbors know each other well enough for a sense of community to develop. Baltimore once had human dimensions, and if Charlie his way, it will one day regain those dimensions.

After dinner, he drives us back to Mount Vernon Hotel, in the city center, but can't resist a slight detour. He tells us to keep our eyes open and let him know if we notice anything strange. Then he turns into the streets of West Baltimore.

Fans of the HBO show *The Wire* would recognize this dreamscape, but seeing it still delivers a numbing shock. Blocks upon blocks of abandoned row houses stand dark, empty, and forbidding, doors and windows boarded up, roofs and ceilings, even rear walls, caving in. Vacant lots break up the monotony and heighten the sense of a vast space, as though the whole city had been left to decay. Charlie points out that the architecture here is identical to that in his plush neighborhood, except that these buildings have been allowed to go to seed. These districts are also organized around squares, which have been stripped of trees and are now dark expanses. The occasional lighted window confirms that a few people still do live here, despite the ruined surroundings. Churches stand within sight of each other, attesting to the communities that once thrived here. Charlie parks his car before a condemned ruin set back from the curb, pointing out the grandness of its design. This wreck was once a mansion with a substantial front garden. He turns a corner, drives a few short blocks, and suddenly we've returned to the city center, where everything is inhabited and pretty once again. Charlie's detour makes his second point clearer: this is a city that has been mangled not just by technological innovation, but also by the responses of city officials and citizens to the problem of race relations.

Once a predominantly white city, Baltimore saw its African-American population grow steadily after the Civil War, as railroads were built and industries requiring a solid labor force were established. Neighborhoods were formed and reformed around skin color, often abetted by zoning policies and development initiatives. West Baltimore became a thriving African-American community, which, as soon as its members could afford to, followed in the footsteps of the previous white residents and relocated to the suburbs. The homes they left behind were taken over by a fresh influx of labor.

Territory began to be marked out, and divisions created, in the form of avenues, boulevards, and highways. Rows of houses were razed in the 1960s to make way for wide throughways that made it difficult and undesirable for residents of West Baltimore to cross over into central Baltimore. These new thoroughfares, in discouraging pedestrian traffic, also discouraged businesses from operating along their lengths, compelling them to set up shop in more central locations on the black side of the city. White residents were thus assured of an insulating layer that separated their "here" from the unpalatable "there." Today, Baltimore is a predominantly black city, and the races still live mostly segregated from each other; according to data from the 2010 census, Baltimore ranks nineteenth on the list of most segregated cities in the United States.

The next morning, we revisit West Baltimore, which seems less malevolent in the light of day. Vacant lots could be mistaken for lawns, and from a distance, the abandoned houses could be any other run-down American neighborhood whose residents are all at work. The stillness, the absence of human activity or vehicular traffic, seems typical of American residential areas, where cold weather drives people indoors, windows shut. The only sign of life is a termite exterminator's truck idling on a corner, its owner trawling the sidewalks for clients. The only businesses that thrive here are pawnshops, funeral parlors, convenience stores, and check cashiers — a kind of banking service for the poor. We walk up and down one of the streets, taking photos: with the appearance of cameras, the tourism framework is superimposed over our visit, and even Charlie can't resist a little pandering — he points further to the west and mentions that the Hamsterdam episodes of *The Wire* were shot there. An urban tragedy slides easily into a spectacle from which one cannot look away.

Ironically, the degeneration of West Baltimore into a ghost town attests to the upward mobility of its former residents, but signifies the deterioration of the city, which no longer has the factories, docks, or mills that attracted new laborers to occupy these houses. The deindustrialization of Baltimore, and the resulting scarcity of jobs, has left these neighborhoods empty. Charlie's solution is to begin attracting fresh immigrants to the city with cheap housing and jobs in the service industry, working for the new urban developments around the harbors. Hispanics, Latinos, and Asians could become this key demographic; today they comprise only five percent of the population, but their numbers could still grow.

Our last few hours in Baltimore are spent bringing the anachronisms full circle. We pass through a luxurious neighborhood of mansions better suited to gated communities or affluent suburbs, just minutes away from downtown. We catch glimpses of the upscale development of the harbor areas, and Johns Hopkins University, the largest employer in the city and perpetrator of more urban development involving the destruction of historic portions of the city. The Baltimore of human dimensions must disappear, it seems, to make room for urban changes that will allow the city to survive. Charlie's cherished idea of what a city should be seems incompatible with current notions of what constitutes progress. Transportation and communication technology have made it unnecessary to crowd into an urban space, which leads to a dispersal of communities, and makes a city truly anonymous, existing to enable only industry and not a way of life. Baltimore is trying to change and adapt to the demands of a new economic environment. Charlie insists that adaptation can happen without changing, or at least without changing in the wrong ways.

As a parting shot, Charlie takes us past one of his favorite developments — the repurposing of factories and warehouses into studio-residences for artists and art students as well as exhibition spaces. The city has managed to attract scores of young creative people to work on their projects in Baltimore and help revitalize its cultural scene. With the new residents come the businesses — groceries and restaurants, galleries and bars, laundromats and department stores — and the cycle of human-based development begins again. Baltimore needs to change, and change need not be the enemy.

MEMPHIS, TENNESSEE

As we fly out of Maryland into Louisiana, I find myself haunted by the desolation of West Baltimore, and I think of the words that came so easily to describe it: ghost town.

Although I'm not sure how or why, the ghost town is a part of my personal American iconography. Perhaps it comes via the few westerns I've watched, or my trip two years ago through the deserts of Utah and Arizona, but there it is: ramshackle, collapsing wooden houses lined up along a dusty, tumbleweed-infested road that goes nowhere in the middle of nowhere. In other parts of the world, there is evidence of larger communities, even civilizations, that abandoned their settlements and disappeared: Angkor, Machu Picchu, Easter Island, Petra. What distinguishes the American ghost town is its small scale — abandoned before it had a chance to grow.

In the westward expansion, American pioneers must have made several false starts, settling in places that proved inhospitable or unlivable after a while. Sometimes the promise of a steady supply of wealth — gold in the river, copper in the hills, oil in the desert — encouraged them to establish actual communities with businesses, public services, and some form of governance before the natural resources were exhausted. Perhaps a railroad line was discontinued, or a highway that had once brought business and customers their way was diverted. Whatever the reason, it was apparently not difficult to pick up and abandon the homes they had built.

Perhaps this is indicative of the American valorization of mobility. Americans move away from home to study, to become adults, to seek their fortune in other states. The pulling up of roots and starting over in a new place are treated as facts of life as inevitable as death, the final settling. The impulse to move is enabled by the size and spaciousness of the country, and the dense web of railroads and highways that criss-cross it. The certainty of a fresh start, a new beginning, bolsters the risk-taking and derring-do of the pioneer spirit and neutralizes the fear of failure. No matter how bad things get, there will always be a car, bus, train, or airplane to take you away to a new beginning.

However, the larger something becomes, the more difficult it becomes to keep things liquid. The ghost towns of the west were small, forgettable, and easy to abandon. Larger communities would take longer to decompose and would be impossible to abandon or eradicate: the persistence of the ruins at Angkor or Machu Picchu, or the unimaginable horror of a deserted Manhattan, so often used for shock effect by Hollywood.

As the infrastructure grows around a community, so does the divide between the city and the people that inhabit it. Over time, a city becomes a living thing in its own right, demanding its own sustenance and maintenance, asserting its own right to exist. When a city flourishes, it can be a beautiful thing that sustains and is sustained by its inhabitants. But because it acquires its own life, it becomes harder to kill and destroy once people decide or are forced to move on. Its scale is no longer human, its dimensions no longer manageable. It will survive, if only as an overgrown ruin, and while it survives, it will continue to remind people of its former existence. There will come a time when people will no longer remember what it meant, and can only resort to speculation on the mystery of an abandoned civilization.

Cities can no longer die. They continue like zombies, decaying shells of what they used to be, lumbering along by force of habit half-remembered. Because existence—the work of living and the upkeep of its standards—has been extended technologically, those who lack the means of keeping up, of starting anew—the under-class—animate the zombie city, sustaining it with just enough inhabitation. The city left behind will not shut down, but will keep on going.

NEW ORLEANS, LOUISIANA

I first visited New Orleans in 1997, staying for ten days to explore the French Quarter and the Garden District. My memories are of a city rapturously alive and strange, as unique an experience as one could find in America.

In 2005, I watched in horror as this lovely city was upended and torn inside out. The misleading coverage by the international media told of an American city reduced to brute savagery, turning on itself in the desperate fight to survive. While I do admit to a tinge of schadenfreude in my reaction, similar to what I felt absorbing the aftermath of 9/11, I could not help but wonder how such helpless chaos could erupt in a country as powerful and as wealthy as the United States. Had America grown so used to the amenities of civilization that it had forgotten how to respond to calamity? As the story of the levee failure began to emerge from behind the cover of Hurricane Katrina, it became clear that the crisis had exposed ruptures in the façade of America, and that something in the American myth had changed forever.

On this trip, I returned to New Orleans with some apprehension, reluctant to displace my glowing memories of the Crescent City. I needed to preserve my experience of a vital, vibrant city that wore her age and colors proudly. As it turns out, I needn't have worried — the places that I had explored in my last visit seemed virtually unchanged. Most of the old restaurants and bars were still there, and those that weren't had been replaced by new ones. The city was packed with people for something called the French Quarter Festival, an annual celebration engineered to bring in more tourism dollars. I saw few to none of the boarded-up store fronts or vacant lots that signaled a city in decline. If anything, the city seemed more aggressively alive than it had ever been, the status quo comfortably restored.

However, the French Quarter and the Garden District had been largely spared by the floods, and the city sprawls over some 350 square miles, home to half a million people before the flood. A streetcar ride through the business district reveals the empty buildings and broken windows of a city reeling from the effects of a natural disaster and an economic downturn. While the tourist center dances on, the rest of the city struggles to keep up.

The city's population dropped to a tenth of its original size after the flood, and only about two-thirds have returned, the rest having decided to relocate permanently in Texas, Utah, and other states where Katrina victims were sent. "Coming back" is a recurrent theme in the city: People need to come back, businesses need to come back, communities need to come back. There continues to be a desire to see the rest of New Orleans restored to a place where people live, not pass through or visit.

We take what's offhandedly referred to as the "disaster tour," a bus ride through the areas hardest hit by the flooding in 2005. It's a grim notion, inviting strangers to gawk at a fresh tragedy, but only because it's fresh—the "Cities of the Dead" have long been a star attraction, and the disaster tour's persistence after five years only attests to the morbid need to rubberneck at an accident, or to view the corpse.

It turns out to be a sterile experience. The tour group remains inside the air-conditioned bus, viewing the sights from behind a sheet of glass, recalling the first images of the flood as delivered on TV screens and computer monitors. As though to remind us, the tour begins with a slide show of photographs, many of them familiar and iconic, of the flood devastation. The tour itself resembles a tram ride through a movie studio's back lots, with its unused standing sets. A rest stop at City Park brings us to a souvenir shop—the ubiquitous exit portal in theme park America. We had hoped that the tour would make what we had read and seen about the flood real, but it has the effect of distancing us further. At one point a resident waves at us from his restored front garden, although he can't see us through the tinted glass of the bus windows. The tour guide explains that he's an informal fixture of the tour now—he has made it a point to greet all the tour buses as they pass. Because we barely slow down to acknowledge him, he's reduced to just another sight to see, an animatronic pirate of the Mississippi.

If anything, the tour's moniker is misleading—much of the devastation that the tour guides tells of is no longer there. Instead, her patter tries to help us visualize the disaster, to superimpose it over neighborhoods that have, slowly but surely, completed their difficult and unpleasant reconstruction. There are traces of the devastation, certainly—empty houses with collapsed roofs, vacant lots, blocks of unoccupied property, hospitals and office buildings abandoned. But time has done its work of healing: grass grows over the vacant lots, giving the empty districts the appearance of a park rather than a wasteland. Hardware stores as large as shopping malls are now the dominant landmarks. However, our guide seems to want more in the way of recovery: the complete restoration of New Orleans as it was before the flood. It is not enough that debris has been disposed of. Homes, residents, and the necessities of a community—food outlets, supply stores, health services, entertainment centers—all these must "come back," and her greatest woe is the creeping possibility that they never will, that New Orleans is now a different city.

Our tour guide unwittingly articulates the impulse to pick up and move on, wishing out loud that homeowners who still lack the means to rebuild after five years would just tear their ruined houses down. She expresses disbelief and mild outrage at the sight of a trailer still parked on the front lawn of an unrestored home. Blight offends the community, and a status quo must be maintained once a reasonable grace period has passed. The majority asserts itself over the individual, who must keep up or be shunned. Implicit in her lament is the uniquely American expectation, even certitude, that something should and will be done to correct an undesirable situation. It's a matter-of-fact attitude that can seriously weaken the ability to adapt, to roll with the punches, preferring instead for the nation, the government, to right the wrong, as it always has. When the system fails, as it did in 2005, such an attitude, clung to so fiercely, so blindly, can result in a spectacle of out-raged helplessness. This was the source of much of the schadenfreude outside America that year: seeing the smug, arrogant declaration "This cannot happen in America" so definitively disproven.

Should the community come back? New Orleans natives cite ties to home and heritage as the strongest reasons for continuing to live in the city. There is too much history and culture in New Orleans to abandon. However, nature is speaking. The Mississippi River has long since wanted to change its course, take a shorter route to the Gulf of Mexico, bypassing the Crescent City. Modifications in the geogra-phy of the region by oil and gas companies have obliterated natural shields against the seasonal torments of hurricanes, and Louisiana is diminished daily as acres of its land are washed into the ocean. Despite the efforts of the Army Corps of Engineers, over the better part of a century, to keep the river in its present configuration and manage the processes of nature, the river laughs and bides its time. Living along the Mississippi delta today is like living in the shadow of a volcano. The denial of the danger is foolhardy, and even the most ingenious precau-tions seem ludicrous.

The homes that have been rebuilt in the flooded areas of New Orleans are now raised on stilts, some to more than twice their original height. The elevations are based on the measured water levels of the flood and calculations of how far beneath sea level the area is. Con-struction companies have devised ways of sliding a flatbed under a home and lifting it, foundation, furniture, and all, the way one would jack up a car to change a tire. The new space under the house becomes a garage, a shaded playground, or a storage area. One such house has been restored into a flat-bottomed barge that can be cut loose to float away if the water rises high enough. In another block rise the houses built by actor and philanthropist Brad Pitt. Attractive and functional, their modern eco-friendly design evokes the colonial architecture of the old neighborhood while leaving a much smaller carbon footprint. Similarly elevated as a defense against flooding, they seem to be more positive examples of how New Orleans might be restored, indulging nostalgia in a clearheaded, sensible way. But just a few hundred yards away, the thin concrete walls of the city levee system stand, marking the source of all-too-near peril. There is a sense that nature has been outwitted yet again here, and this remains a dangerous belief to invest in.

New Orleans stands at an uneasy, critical juncture. It's a city that has grown roots, according to the expediencies of geographical and environmental conditions of a time past. Over the years, it has resisted nature, attempting to bend bodies of water to its will. The triumph of a few decades, or a few centuries, can seem like a triumph for all time, but it is all too easy to be lulled into mistaking the present for the boundless future, in which decades, even centuries, can become insignificant.

In the meantime, human lives and family histories exert a strong pull. Many New Orleans natives chose to come back because their memories, and their ancestors' memories, can offer no alternatives. "My family has always lived here" is a common rationale, against which few would be willing to argue. Furthermore, the city's singular character and its cultural heritage—as the birthplace of jazz, for instance—make it doubly difficult to surrender to the processes of nature. Historically, New Orleans has always been vigorously defended against destruction—by disease, fire, and natural calamity. It is a city that has always had to fight for its survival. Now it is waging a war against an inexorable primal force, and many have and will come to its defense.

How much will have to be sacrificed for New Orleans? Rural farmland is flooded, and towns are relocated to ensure the survival of this city and others further up the banks of the Mississippi. New Orleans may continue to celebrate Mardi Gras each year, but first the beads, sequins, and feathers must be washed clean of blood.

MORGAN CITY AND LAFAYETTE, LOUISIANA

Out of New Orleans, we drive west to Morgan City, on the banks of the Atchafalaya River. Our main destination here is Mr. Charlie, a transportable, submersible offshore drilling rig, the first of its kind, built in 1954, decommissioned in 1986, and now converted into a museum. Tour groups walk through the rig, listening to a man who used to work on it and now volunteers as a tour guide.

The rig is a massive metal contraption, essentially a giant barge that floats to where the oil is and extends its legs to the ocean floor, enabling it to drill wells and install pipes to extract oil. The scale of the machine overwhelms its visitors, who climb onto it via a series of metal staircases and gangways. Apart from the drilling machinery and power generators, the rig also includes living quarters for up to fifty-eight crew members. Designed to be an "independent island," it allows people to work offshore for up to forty-five days at a time.

The tour is organized around showing how the crew lived and worked on the rig, which has been set up to appear fully functional, as though its workers had just gone ashore on furlough. The living quarters are empty, but clean and ready for occupancy. Their staterooms are windowless and cramped, with a spare, military aesthetic, reminding one of a battleship. In the mess hall, signs still offer advice on proper dining attire and behavior. Utensils lie waiting in bins, and ladles and pots hang from hooks over gleaming stainless steel counters. The recreation room features a moody painting in the Ashcan School style of oil rig workers at work. There's a foosball table, packs of cards and dominoes, a VCR, and a television. On a coffee table between two lumpy couches are two Bibles—one a generic edition of the Gideon variety, the other something called *God's Word for the Oil Patch: Fuel for the Soul.*

The presence of long-gone workers hovers in the musty air, hugging the artifacts of their life on this rig. Sharing the dangerous and difficult labor of operating the rig must have fostered a powerful sense of camaraderie, which lingers in these empty rooms like a smell. It's not hard to imagine them bonding into a community and then extending that community beyond the rig to the families that they support. The hard labor of extracting a precious commodity that an entire nation depends on cultivates a strong pride in their contribution to society, as well as a fierce loyalty to the company that keeps them and their families alive. In this part of Louisiana, it is difficult to keep a conversation about the detrimental effects of the petroleum industry from degenerating into an argument.

Further north, in Lafayette, the pastor of a Christian church candidly admits, "We all work for the oil companies," referring to his flock, as well as to the other residents of Southern Louisiana. His sermon earlier that morning laid out a plan in seven bullet points for dealing with transitions and changes. He is virile and charismatic, and it's easy to get caught up in his inspirational fervor. He is aware that the members of his congregation are undergoing difficult times, with the recession compounded by the increased scrutiny and regulation of the oil industry following the environmental disaster of the BP oil spill in 2010. On this day, he has selected the opening verses from the Book of Joshua, in which Yahweh tells Joshua to prepare the Chosen People for the Promised Land. With some rhetorical sleight of hand, the Israelites become this congregation, and Yahweh's promises to Joshua become God's promises to the people of Lafayette. The mood is tribal, and the tone is aggressive. This pastor is not just a spiritual leader; he is also self-help guru, life coach, and cheerleader, preaching tough love via PowerPoint.

The same Old Testament aggression seems to animate Mr. Charlie, a man-made machine designed to wrest natural resources from the earth. As I stand on its deck, I imagine it moving down the Atchafalaya to the Gulf of Mexico, a mythical behemoth preparing to bend nature to its will. The innards of its machinery—the drill bits, chains, cables, rivets, booms, pipes—their cold hardness thrums with their power to maim and annihilate. Hard hats aren't required on the drilling platform, because they offer no protection against that power. The oil rig, born of human industry, enabled by the divine mandate of dominion over creation, signifies nothing less than the hand of God moving visibly on Earth, even now as it sits in its final resting place.

On the other hand, it is an all-too-fallible invention. The BP oil spill began with an explosion that killed eleven crew members on the Deepwater Horizon rig. The resulting fire could not be controlled, and after thirty-six hours, the rig capsized and sank five thousand feet to the ocean floor. The well drilling gushed continuously for almost three months, drenching miles of coastline and acres of wetland in crude oil. The machine capable of awesome work also wreaks awesome damage.

The communities loyal to the oil industry are quick to downplay the event, labeling it an accident, thereby absolving humans and institutions of culpability. Beyond the accidental, however, is the undeniable incidental damage that has already been done by oil and gas companies to the geography and ecosystem of Louisiana. Waterways in the bayou have been indiscriminately widened to allow their rigs, barges, and other water vehicles to travel between the Gulf and their inland docks and plants. Acres of wetlands have been denuded, exposing the southern coast of Louisiana to the full force of hurricanes and to the dangers of flooding. Silting and sedimentation raise the water levels in the bayous and river basins and degrade the water quality, killing the fish that provide livelihood for fishermen. Worst of all, the coastline of Louisiana is being lost to erosion at an alarming rate. Communities have already been displaced by the disappearing land, but no outcry has been sounded, perhaps because the numbers and demographics are too insignificant to matter. The Cajuns of Louisiana, who number about seven hundred fifty thousand distributed over sixty-four parishes, have been fighting a legal battle with the oil companies for the last five years over the destruction of the ecosystem off which they eke out a living, though nature will easily outpace the legal system.

It is by no means a simple case of David versus Goliath, as many Cajuns also work for the oil companies. The man who designed Mr. Charlie, and thereby revolutionized the petroleum industry, was of Cajun stock, and the industry itself, at least in Louisiana, is identified as Cajun-born.

It's easy to imagine shifting one's allegiance to the oil rig. Hard, honest, dangerous labor to provide a natural resource that is the source of and key ingredient for a wide variety of products can seem like a noble, honorable way to live. One can romanticize this labor force as the back-bone of American society, even as these jobs put food on tables and provide energy to a country that will collapse without its fossil fuels and natural gases. The pastor guiding his flock through the dark times is inspired not by mere optimism, but by the certainty that his coun-try cannot afford to give this industry up, or at least cannot imagine a future without its bounty. In the harsh desert world of the Old Testa-ment, far more terrible sacrifices are made to claim one's divine birth-right. Keep your eye on God's presence, and on God's promises, the pastor concludes. In the quiet bowels of Mr. Charlie, I hear the echo of this abiding faith in the rewards that will come to those who do God's work on earth.

BREAUX BRIDGE, LOUISIANA

There's a long drive from our cabins at Breaux Bridge to the boat ramp at Bayou Benoit from which we're to set out on a tour of the Atcha-falaya River Basin and its system of bayous. We travel along a narrow slithering road at the foot of a tall, long, unnaturally even, grassy ridge, atop which cars and trucks speed in the opposite direction. We realize, belatedly, that these sloping ridges are the levees that keep the river basin on the other side from spilling over. They're a far cry from the comparatively puny concrete and steel walls that engird New Orleans. These earthen mounds, even if they are man-made, appear more of a piece with nature, and thereby better equipped to deal with it. In the heart of Cajun country, the control of nature is also crucial to survival, although human intervention often does worse damage.

Our guides are a trio of white-haired men in the last stages of middle age, but they exude a strength, vitality, and confidence that goes well with their years. They pile us into a trio of small flat-bottomed motor-boats, and take us through the twists and turns of the bayou network. One of the boats has been outfitted with concessions to comfort—forward-facing garden chairs on a swath of faded carpet.

A boat ramp descends into the water, designed to allow the easy lowering of a boat on a trailer via a gentle incline. What seems like a cumbersome, strenuous task is achieved efficiently in a matter of minutes. Soon our boats are cruising down a foliage-lined waterway that widens and opens into a vast lake, its horizon just visible in the distance. The basin evokes visions of a watery apocalypse, the end of the world by deluge. Out of the expanse of muddy water rise dead or dying trees, their only foliage ropes of Spanish moss. Inland are patches of marshy ground, out of which thicker clumps of trees grow, with waterways snaking through. In some places, a fetid miasma hangs over the water, marking already stagnant areas. What had once been a dense cypress forest has been progressively denuded by loggers since after the Civil War, leaving only stumps and hollow trees by 1929. Flooding brought about by efforts to maintain the Mississippi River's path submerged the forest, creating an eerie swamp-scape that continues to change due to sedimentation. An ecosystem died, and a new watery one has emerged in its place, acquiring over time its own desolate beauty.

There is a touristy aspect to our ride—we are taken up close to particularly gnarled and weathered cypress trees, weaving through carpets of alligator grass—a combination of water hyacinth, hydrilla, and salvinia—and encouraged to pluck at dangling tendrils of Spanish moss and pungent cypress fruit. A beaver or nutria sighting necessitates a detour for a closer view. Ospreys are pointed out, and we are told to seek out the nearby aeries, usually perched atop the tallest, most inaccessible tree in the vicinity. A few nets, traps, and fishing lines are hauled up. In one, a gigantic catfish, at least three feet long, whips and thrashes. A crawfish trap yields only two, and this fact is shared between the boats above the sound of the motors. Some nets come up empty, and there's no surprise or dismay. There are some fretful remarks about why there has been no alligator sighting yet, tinged with worry that this star attraction still has not made an appearance, and there's a palpable relief and gratification when the first one, just a baby, is spotted.

These boatmen, Cajuns all and natives to the bayou, seem to know what their audience wants to see. This landscape is familiar to them, but they have learned to see it with outsider's eyes as well, identifying the exotic and enticing, the better to satisfy visitors and encourage more to come. They are indulgent with us, answering our questions, preening for our benefit, and pleased, or amused, when we respond with awe and enthusiasm. It's a warm and affable performance, built upon what seems to be a heartfelt fondness for the bayou, and a fierce pride in their ability to master it.

There was a time when a substantial living could be made off the bayou, and our tour guides are old enough to remember. But environmental changes, cultural shifts, and human intervention in natural processes are working against the Cajun way of life. Small wonder that it appears to be an aging population. At Mulate's, a popular local restaurant, the crowd is predominantly senior citizens, with just a smattering of younger parents with their children. The teenage to twenty-something set is conspicuously absent, save for the service staff and the band, which plays the zydeco to which only the older patrons dance. The younger generation have moved away to other cities or states, or are working in nontraditional jobs, such as in the oil industry, understanding that to remain a traditional Cajun is to be poor in a country that has moved on. While it's true that Cajun families own the property they live on and the infrastructure of their livelihood, the bayou can no longer sustain an American lifestyle the way it used to. America has moved away from nature, altering the models for standards of living, which are now incompatible with the Cajun lifestyle.

The traditional sources of income for Cajuns have been turned unfashionable, obsolete, illegal, or unsustainable by the march of progress. Concern for animal welfare has rendered fur trapping no longer viable, as with killing alligators for their meat and skins. Spanish moss, once in great demand for upholstery and mattress stuffing, has been replaced by synthetic hypoallergenic material. Fishing in the Atchafalaya Basin, an exclusively Cajun activity, is now an unproductive industry because of sedimentation, poor water quality, and intense competition from Chinese and Vietnamese imports. The wheels of progress in Louisiana are driven by the oil and chemical industries — large-scale businesses that generate sizable incomes and supply essential needs for the rest of the country. Urban America has little use for small-scale, rural enterprises, and distances itself from the violence of living so close to nature.

To be sure, Cajuns are no saintly environmentalists. Their motorboats produce carbon monoxide, disturb the bayou floor, and leak poison into the water, and they are predators to all the wildlife in the ecosystem. They straddle the tops of the food chains with impunity, in the Judeo-Christian tradition of humans as stewards of creation. While they romanticize their relationship with nature in a transcendental, Thoreau-infused way, they clearly see themselves as separate from it, living off it but not of it. The Choctaw, who named the Atchafalaya ("long river" in their language), would have been mindful of the river's selfhood and its presence as a shaping, even sacred, force in their universe. However, the real question here is one of scale — even as a community, the Cajuns have had neither the will nor the ability to deplete the bayou's resources. Only the arrival of larger industries — logging and oil, especially — has threatened this way of life, altering the environment it depends on.

On the way back to our cabins, we stop at the home of one of our tour guides, who graciously allows us to wander over his property. The house is modest and functional, and the aesthetic rough-hewn. A hundred yards away, past the tree-shaded backyard, a small dock extends into the bayou, which throws back the afternoon sun. The front yard is pleasantly cluttered with discarded kitchenware, equipment, tools, seedling boxes, bags of fertilizer, and water containers of various sizes. In the garden, handmade wind chimes tinkle in the branches. The stars and stripes fly proudly from the peaked roof of a garage. Below, nailed to the façade, are the skulls of two alligators and at least twenty deer, some with only two-pointed antlers. In a water drum nearby is a turtle, its shell almost two feet long, waiting to be made into soup.

Inside the house, on the living room walls, hang framed family photos — parents, wife, children, and grandchildren, in various stages of maturation. Here at last is the invisible generation, the younger one that learned the ways of the bayou from parent and grandparent, but no longer speaks the exclusively oral Cajun French, or aspires to continue living the Cajun life. Here is the generation that was born on the bayou, but has grown away from it. Here is the generation that has seen the future of Louisiana and of America, and has decided to catch up. In their photos, Cajun men and women age, but their companions — posing with them in boats, on a riverbank, beside a prize catch — remain young: children who disappear after the yearbook photo, and who beget grandchildren who take their place beside grandpa and grandma, spending a summer or Thanksgiving with them before returning to their newer homes and more modern lifestyles.

Ultimately, the survival of Cajun culture might be in the form of a tourist attraction — quaint oddities on display for "les Americains," the tourists who come to gawk at the exotic as it is performed for them. Greg Guirard, Cajun author, historian, and activist, writes, "I don't want to see Cajun Country turn into a synthetic Cajun theme park. I don't want to see our homeland converted into just another roadside attraction." These days, however, with the bayou ecosystem irreversibly altered, there might be more of a living in pandering to tourists than in fishing. Cajun cuisine and music have already been appropriated in New Orleans, the tourist mecca of Louisiana. All over the state are bed-and-breakfasts and hotels offering an "authentic" bayou experience. The cabin complex where we spend the night features former homes and outhouses transplanted plank by plank next to the bayou, restored to habitable condition, and decorated with amiable antique clutter. The kitchen serves homemade boudin, cracklings, and cheese, and the establishment's atmosphere is aggressively laid-back. As with the boat ride, it's an affable, proud performance, one that harbors no resentment towards the crazy folk who have come to stare at the natives. They enjoy their difference, after all, and assert it cheerfully.

Within the larger context, however, the Cajun community does not seem to count, beyond its eccentric culture. In May 2011, the world watched as swaths of Cajun country were deliberately flooded to protect large industry-driven cities such as Baton Rouge and New Orleans from the dangerously swelling Mississippi. Priorities have been set, and those without political or economic power were selected to take one for the team. Homeowners raised their voices as they evacuated in tears, while others dug in, fortifying their property. As in the past, whole communities have been forced to relocate because of environmental changes, but the changes wrought by human intervention are more bitter. Those who have moved away return yearly for reunions in the old country, but sooner or later, traditions will be forgotten as the past becomes more distant. The time will come when no one will remember what it was like to live on the bayou, having never lived on it. Monuments are erected over the dead, and this community has yet to declare itself defeated, all evidence to the contrary.

As urban and suburban culture homogenizes America (and the world), perhaps the way of all Americana is the museum or the theme park. Culture will be honored through memorialization, but it will have to die in the process.

ATLANTA, GEORGIA

The Delta Airlines hub in Atlanta swirls with people. It recalls rush hour in a downtown area: streams of people pushing past each other, café tables full, with more customers lining up to place their orders. Trains are necessary to transport passengers from one terminal to another, so large is this space whose main function is that of transit junction. Most of the people are not even coming from Atlanta or disembarking here—they're just passing through, part of the airline's regular operations. As the workday winds down, the crowds diminish, shops close, the sound of airplanes comes less frequently, and the different components of this center start shutting down for the night. Soon this space will be closed to traffic for a few hours, before starting up again. Next to New Orleans at the height of the annual French Quarter Festival, airports have seemed the most densely populated parts of America on this trip. So this is where all the people are.

Airline hubs—a way of making air travel more efficient and profitable—are yet another manifestation of the sort of assembly line approach to operations with which America is often associated. While this might have been inspired by or borrowed from European practices, in America is has been applied to every industry—from the kitchens of McDonalds to the factories of Detroit to the warehouses of Amazon. The same principle of piecemeal work on standardized components now operates in the herding of passengers into dispatching centers, where they are fed through systematic security checks, filtered according to destination, and sent on their way. Passengers undergo the same process as their luggage—scanned, classified, tagged, loaded, and unloaded. Airplanes queue neatly for their turns at the takeoff runway, and at a properly functioning airport, the most gratifying sound will be the regular roaring of jets taking off or landing.

It's emblematic of how American society is structured around travel and mobility. If the invention of the car led to the invention of the suburb, the invention of the airplane led to the establishment of a national business network, one based in major cities defined by the size and capabilities of their airports, and connected by the standard routes of air travel. While this shrank the country, it also had the effect of allowing a population to disperse across the breadth of the states. No longer was there a need to crowd into New York or the East Coast to establish a business. One chooses a location based on its convenience and flies in and out as necessary. A major news organization can set up shop in Georgia, an electronics industry can blossom in California, and a courier service can operate out of Tennessee. Even the rise of the Internet has not diminished air traffic; in some ways it has increased it.

Models have been proposed for societies structured around airports, the way little economies sprout around train stations and subway terminals. The airport city would be a transient city—people would stay for short periods of time to conduct business before flying off to other destinations or driving out to a home in the suburbs. Like an airport, but on an even larger scale, the city would wind down at certain hours of the day, or certain days of the week, or certain holidays of the year, becoming virtual temporary ghost towns. The rest of the time, as a transit hub, it becomes as alive and busy as anyone's idea of a city.

BIRMINGHAM, ALABAMA

The northwestern sector of downtown Birmingham seems trapped in the early 1960s, futuristic Art Deco architecture and all. It isn't a deliberate preservation effort; nor has the area gone to seed. It just seems as though progress decided to stop moving through this place, keeping the sandwich joints and barber shops just the way they were. Whatever the intention, it has the effect of evoking the racially charged atmosphere of the years of the African-American Civil Rights Movement, which succeeded in introducing anti-discrimination laws to American legislation, but only after a long and bloody process.

Although Birmingham was established after the Civil War as an industrial, rather than agricultural, city, Jim Crow segregation laws enforced strict divisions between races. As recently as forty years ago, the African-American community lived apart from the white community in Birmingham, in their own neighborhoods with their own commercial centers. In this neighborhood in downtown Birmingham, a few streets have remained unchanged, their original homes and buildings still standing. The lower, flatter, and more modest architecture contrasts with that of the business district, with its blocks of grandiose, massive skyscrapers that showcase the metals manufacturing industry the city was founded upon. There are some efforts to preserve the black neighborhood as a historic site, although it continues to be an active neighborhood, where people live and work. However, such a move feels inappropriate, even to an outsider. While there is a need to carry the memory of injustice forward, preserving a segregated neighborhood, whose existence and appearance was brought about and shaped by injustice, seems to negate the principles of desegregation. Still, Birmingham continues to be one of the most segregated cities in America, although great strides have been made in terms of increased tolerance, respect, and the intermingling of races. Now a predominantly black city, it seems unsure of how to handle its controversial history.

The Kelly Ingram Park, for instance, once the site of civil rights demonstrations and violent dispersals, most famously of school-age children menaced by attack dogs and fire hoses, features memorials to that infamy. Sharp-toothed, misshapen hounds lunge out of monoliths on either side of a walkway; a boy and a girl stand defiantly behind prison bars; water cannons aim at two cowering people. The statues, nightmarish and grim, bind the park to the history, precluding any other use of that space. Across the street, the Civil Rights Institute is a research center and museum whose main attraction is a multimedia exhibit detailing the history of the movement. The details of the exhibit have been subject to much argument and protest over which version of the story to present or highlight, or if the exhibit should even tell the story at all.

Birmingham, once known as Bombingham due to the rash of anti-black bombings in the 1950s and 60s, initially did not attract as much national attention as other key cities in the movement. That changed with the bombing of the 16th Street Baptist Church on September 15, 1963, which claimed the lives of four young girls. So outrageous and shocking was this incident that the murders of two black boys elsewhere in the city on the same day have been virtually forgotten. This bombing is credited by many to be the galvanizing moment in the Civil Rights Movement, providing the momentum for the final push to its victory.

Almost as old as Birmingham itself, the church continues to minister to its mostly black congregation over one hundred thirty years after it was established to serve the needs of the black laborers who came to work in the mines, foundries, factories, and railroads. The brick structure on 16th Street, completed in 1911, is undergoing repair work on the day we visit, and there is no service, but a volunteer tour guide walks us through the sanctuary. T.R. German lived through the days of segregation in Alabama, and fought in a segregated military unit during the Korean War. He offers up a few anecdotes about discrimination, but he waves our questions about contemporary race relations aside, steering the conversation to Jesus Christ's gospel of love and understanding. To him, there are larger national concerns than race, and he may be right: "The devil is busy." What is especially striking, however, is the way in which the Christian rhetoric spouted here differs from that pervading the church we visited in Louisiana.

Christianity was introduced to African-American slaves as a way of subjugating them, but they quickly found in it a message of hope — the promise of redemption after a long period of suffering. This is virtually the same message of the Louisiana pastor's sermon, but here the tone is meek rather than defiant, patient rather than aggressive, more

New Testament than Old. The centerpiece of the church is the Wales Window, a stained glass depiction of a dark-skinned Christ figure in a cruciform pose, head bowed, one hand extended to block evil and danger, the other reaching out for mercy and forgiveness. The Chosen People are also reincarnated in this black congregation, but their entitlement lies in the afterlife, and they can only wait and practice love, forgiveness, and understanding in this one. These Christians are likelier to turn the other cheek than to demand an eye for an eye.

T.R. leads us into the church basement, which functions as a Sunday school venue and a community hall. The area where the bomb exploded is now a kitchen, but the tragedy is remembered in a narrow exhibit room at the back of the hall, with framed photographs and newspaper clippings, commemorative plaques, the altar and Bible in the church that day, bits of rubble, and the clock that stopped at the moment the bomb went off. T.R. points out a woman at work in the hall, whom he says was related to one of the girls who died. He introduces us to a friend who lived in the city in the 1960s. However, there are no stories forthcoming. In the face of this fresh memory, reticence seems the respectful response.

Despite the exhibit and the guided tour, this Church resists becoming a museum, insisting on its continued vitality and contribution to the well-being of its congregation. Although the Jim Crow laws were repealed decades ago, relations between blacks and whites in Birmingham remain tense, and there is still much work to be done. T.R. says, "It's a taught thing," referring both to racism and to respect. The process of education can be slow, and perhaps it will take one more generation, or four, to forget the mindsets and world views that enabled slavery and segregation.

The students of a creative nonfiction writing class at the University of Alabama in Birmingham betray some discomfort when they are asked about how the history of their city and their state affects them and their writing. They express reluctance to engage race issues in their nonfiction pieces, although they are aware of them. Of greater concern is how that history has crystallized an unpleasant image of their city and their state, because like any stereotype, it is incomplete and simplistic. The generation represented by these students might still be too near to that history; some of them might be related to surviving members of the Ku Klux Klan, and to delve into a potentially ugly aspect of their heritage might be too much to handle at this point in their lives.

One of the more chilling exhibits at the Civil Rights Institute is a Klansman's robe and hood. Tactfully mounted on a wall, rather than worn by a mannequin, its size suggests a diminutive owner. A card beside it tells us it arrived there courtesy of an anonymous donor.

While we were in Birmingham, a local black newspaper reported the death of a young black man in a neighboring city. Because the circumstances of the death recall and suggest a lynching, the newspaper saw fit to make this the banner story, and splashed a gruesome close-up of the hanged man on its upper fold, while downplaying the possibility that it might have been a suicide.

Beyond the racial tension, Birmingham is also a city in trouble. Banking and insurance replaced mining and manufacturing as its key industries, leaving the city especially vulnerable to the recession. The downtown area is quiet and traffic-free on a weekday, and many of the skyscrapers stand almost empty. As we walk through town, we pass empty parking lots and storefronts, dusty windows displaying For Rent signs. Restaurants are few and far between. The downtown activity is now concentrated in the south, where the University of Alabama occupies several city blocks and is the city's largest employer, similar to Baltimore. The population might not have fled yet to better prospects in other states, but it's easy to forget that, standing on a sidewalk in the business district at rush hour, not another soul in sight.

WASHINGTON, DC

By the time our tour group arrives in Washington, DC, we are overwhelmed and exhausted. The last stop on our two-week itinerary is a walk through Arlington National Cemetery, which brings our tour full circle to the Civil War.

This cemetery grew around the graves of refugee slaves and Civil War dead buried at the doorstep of Robert E. Lee, on his sequestered plantation—a slap in his face for his betrayal of the Union. Since then, graves have blossomed outwards, sprawling over the sequestered plantation, to include memorials to the dead from every major war America has been involved in, as well as presidents, military heroes, supreme court justices, scientists, and athletes. The design of the cemetery is stark and somber. The graves, marked by white crosses, are arranged in neat, symmetrical rows that follow the curves of the earth, echoing regiment formations. An oppressive neatness pervades, even when it is disrupted by vivid swaths of tulips. It is a sterile, manicured environment in which the smoke, dust, and blood of battle, and the messiness of even the most unremarkable of deaths, is stripped of its chaos, cleansed, and redeemed. An aesthetic triumph over oblivion enables the survivors to continue living.

Outside the cemetery's visitors' center, I overhear a harried father herding his wife and two young children towards the Metro station entrance. "We need to go see the Lincoln Memorial now, if we're going to make it to the Jefferson before dinner." I follow them down the steep and impossibly long escalator that descends to the trains. The DC Metro system runs deep underground in cavernous, vaulted tunnels that recall Quonset huts, air raid shelters, or crypts.

It's here that I begin to sense a semi-accidental symmetry in the design of this study tour, as it ends in the capital of the United States. In many ways, it is a living, prosperous city, perhaps the only American city impervious to crises and disasters. As the seat of governance and political power, it must rank highest amongst national priorities, the last city to go, were the United States to collapse. Citizens live and work here, some with families that go back for generations. Those who relocate are soon replaced. If America moves, the epicenter of its movement is in Washington, DC.

However, to non-residents, it can appear completely different. Its attractions tend to revolve around the themes of history and death. Tourists visiting Washington are usually directed to its monuments and memorials, most commemorating historical figures, historical events, or heroes who gave their lives for the country. An alternative choice are the city's many museums, which are essentially mausoleums housing relics and artifacts of bygone eras. Government institutions and the structures that house them—the White House, the Capitol, the Library of Congress, the U.S. Mint—might all be vital spaces, but are presented to visitors as historical museums or exhibitions of the artifacts of political power. Because the experience of visiting Washington is thus codified, the city becomes yet another iteration of Disneyland—self-contained, fabricated, and organized around a series of attractions celebrating various versions of death. In it, theme park and cemetery are fused, graves and mausoleums become the main attractions, and the city wraps itself around the spectacle, heedlessly celebrating its life as though it had discovered the key to survival.

MINNEAPOLIS/ST. PAUL, MINNESOTA

On my flight back to the Philippines, I found myself seated next to a young Maryland native of Puerto Rican descent, also on his way to Manila. He had noticed my Philippine passport and asked if I knew what was required of a foreigner wanting to apply for one. I didn't.

As it turned out, he was taking this trip, his first outside America, to meet a Filipina he had met on the Internet five years ago. Their webcam-enabled relationship was more tempestuous than most, owing partly to an eight-year age gap, and to her capricious, jealous nature. "She's like a little girl," he says affectionately. He had been sending her gifts and money, even putting her through nursing school, realizing that the dollars he received as a building superintendent and handyman went a long way in the Philippines. The vague plan was to have her migrate to America as a nurse and live happily ever after with him.

However, now that she had completed her course of study, she was refusing to take the board exams for murky reasons, and insisting that he send more cash anyway. Because there had been indications in the past that he might not be the only benefactor in her life, he had decided to go on this adventure to see once and for all if there was anything to this relationship.

It was a familiar enough scenario, except that he, at thirty, was at least twenty years younger than the usual suitor, and the wrong race. Rather than ordering a bride through a web site, hundreds of white men from America, Europe, and Australia, divorced and retired, have instead found other ways to strike up long-distance friendships with countless Filipinas, hope fueling the correspondence on both sides. The desire to find a young, submissive, hardworking, exotic wife is matched with the need for a better life, one far away from the dead-end swelter of a developing country. From an outsider's perspective, it's easy to color such a transaction sad and desperate, but if both parties get what they want or need, what room is left for sadness, tradeoffs notwithstanding?

He didn't seem at all sad or desperate, just excited, and maybe a little scared of embarking on this adventure. He had kept his options open, and I learned that he had made other Filipina webcam friends, with whom he was still in touch. He sends them cash and gifts freely, ingenuously, and doesn't seem to expect anything in return. I almost want to give him a good shake and try to talk some sense into him.

There's a kindness that masks a need to rescue, to assist, to intervene. I see it often in visitors to the Philippines, who are overwhelmed by the poverty and immediately reach out to help, by giving food or money to the nearest beggar. On the other hand, I don't sense the same kind of sympathy proffered freely to the poor and homeless in America, who seem expected to bootstrap themselves out of their circumstances, sooner rather than later. This kindness could be another expression of economic, even racial, superiority, or perhaps a benign sort of messianic tendency. But it does leave one wide open to exploitation, even this fellow with his limited means. As we chat some more, I nudge the conversation towards what is to me an obvious question. Cautiously, I ask him if he's sure she's not just taking advantage of him.

I'm relieved when he doesn't take my prying the wrong way, and more so when he admits that the thought has crossed his mind.

He tells me that in his research on the Philippines he came upon one of the more popular creation myths—that of Tungkung Langit and Alunsina, two divine beings, male and female, who live in the universe before anything else came into being. Tungkung Langit, proprietor of creation, is constantly traveling to do his job, while Alunsina stays home tending her hair and imagining jealous scenarios about what her lover might be up to. When he discovers that she sent the sea breeze to spy on him and report on his activities, a lovers' quarrel ensues. Alunsina storms off in a huff. Tungkung Langit, repentant and lonely, seeks her out but can't find her. Ages pass. He creates the world, makes it beautiful, to entice her to return. He hangs her mirror and comb in the sky and scatters her jewels across the firmament (creating sun, moon, and stars), hoping that she'll see them and come back. She never does, and he continues wandering the universe in search of her, shedding his tears as rain over the earth.

There's much to be said about a society that believes that the universe was born out of a failed romance, but there are more immediate parallels, which my seatmate recognizes. He laughs ruefully and shakes his head.

"There's a high probability that this won't end well," I tell him. "So are you prepared to wander the universe in tears?"

"We'll see," he replies. He'd much rather have that than face a lingering "what-if" in his life, he explains. He glances at the book in my lap and smirks. It's called *The American Future*.

We part ways in Minneapolis, and I don't see him again until Manila. I spend the rest of my journey thinking about Philippine history, and how my country had been purchased from Spain by America, along with Guam and Puerto Rico, for twenty million dollars.

As I make my way to the taxi stand, I see him in the distance — a big burly dude dragging a plastic-encased suitcase in a floral pattern, struggling with his floppy duffel bag and cellphone. He's walking away from the airport taxis that I recommended, and I remember that his girlfriend promised to pick him up with her family, probably in a rented jeepney, as per Filipino custom. "Greeters" are sequestered in a special area away from the terminal exit, so he has a little bit more to go on his journey.

Belatedly I wonder if I should have given him my contact information, just in case. The last thing my country needs is another tourist leaving with bad memories. I call out his name, but he doesn't hear. His chin juts forward, leading the way, and he's shuffling quickly, urgently, towards the greeters' area, dodging passing shuttles and taxis.

That's that, I think, and I hail my own cab.

EDUARDO HALFÓN

Pastoral Scene of the Gallant South

A LOVE STORY

I'd been to Gettysburg before. I was perhaps twelve or thirteen years old and can't really remember much more than a cheap hotel, and all twenty or so junior high students meeting late at night in the room of a girl named Betsy—to smoke and cavort and play spin-the-bottle and Ouija board. But nothing much happened, I don't think. No kisses. A little hand-holding. Very few ghosts. This time, almost thirty years later, we also stayed at a cheap hotel, we also tried to contact ghosts—through the booming ghost-tour business—but we didn't meet late at night to play anything, I don't think.

Eight international writers in Gettysburg to begin "a study tour of the Mid-Atlantic and the American South," they said, "to explore the theme of fall and recovery in America." They called it Writers in Motion. Catchy title. As opposed, I thought when I first read it, to writers who aren't in motion, who remain still. A Guatemalan author once told me that, in his opinion, there were two types of writers: those deep in life, and those deep in their room.

A private van picked us up early the first morning to go out to the battlefields with Peter Carmichael, director of the Civil War Institute and professor of Civil War Studies at Gettysburg College, and any cynicism I might have had—and I certainly had some— started to dissipate as soon as we stepped onto a grave.

Well, not really a grave. It could have been a grave. It looked like a grave, anyway, with a ring of dry logs deliberately placed to resemble a Civil War burial site. But it didn't feel like one until Professor Carmichael handed out some photocopies and we started reading out loud the letters of one John Futch, Union soldier from Company K, third Regiment, out of New Hanover, Connecticut.

The syntax and grammar of his letters was baffling, arcane, almost unreadable. Their emotion and truthfulness, however, were not. John Futch, we soon learned from Professor Carmichael, was illiterate.

In a letter to his wife from Bunker Hill, dated July 19, 1863, he dictated to a stenographer news of his brother's recent death: "Charly got kild and he suffered a graideal from his wound he lived a night and a day after he was woundid we sead hard times thare but we got a nugh to eat ther but we dont now as to my self I get a nugh for I dont want nothing to eat hardly for I am all must sick all the time and half crazy."

In another letter to his wife, dated August 6, 1863, again he dictated of his brother's death to a stenographer, probably a different stenographer: "You expressed a desire To know the particulars of Brother Charlys death I will endeavor to give them to you as well as I can When our Regt charged the enemies entrenchments on the near Gettysburg Pa on the night of July the 3d he was wounded on or near the top of his head it did not pass through the brain but I think it must have bruised them as he did not speak after he was hit he was lying down loading at the time I carried him out he seemed anxious to talk to me but could not He lingered till about two oclock on the 3d when he died. I remained with him from the time he was wounded until he died we buried him on the night of the 3d Only God knows the bitter anguish this sad bereavement sent thrilling through my sad heart."

Two stenographers. Two styles. Same narrative, same narrator even. And yet the language differed, which, in turn, somehow changed the story being told, or its tone, or at least its appearance. Stenography. Narrow writing. From the Greek words *stenos* (narrow) and *graphe* (writing). Isn't a writer a kind of stenographer? Isn't literature also a type of narrow writing? To tell a story narrowly? To craft a narrative by the slimmest of margins? Doesn't a writer also take dictation from an illiterate voice, sometimes external, other times from within? Doesn't a writer give written words to that which is unwritten, even unwritable?

John Futch, we were then told by Professor Carmichael as we stood around the ring of old logs, deserted the Union Army in September of 1863. He was soon after captured, court-martialed, and executed for desertion with a shot to the head.

I have no conclusion here. Not really. Just a feeling of despair. Just a lingering image of an illiterate soldier shot once through the head. And another image of a man digging a shallow ditch in the earth to bury his brother. And another image of his hand-written story, jotted down by another soldier's hand, on yellowish paper, in sad black ink.

Still holding the photocopies of those letters, still standing next to a phony grave, I glanced up at all the perfectly placed trees, all the oaks and cedars and poplars that were and weren't supposed to be there: some planted and others cut down, we were being told by Professor Carmichael, to give the battlefield a Civil War look. I then remembered a childhood tree we used to climb with my brother. I started thinking about my own brother—the intimacy and love, the fist fights and childhood rivalries, all the unkind words that never fade, that haven't faded, that have remained floating in the air like bad smells. I stopped thinking about it. I stopped listening to Professor Carmichael talking about the trees. I suddenly felt anger toward something, but I couldn't say what. And I recalled reading about *litost*.

It's a Czech word. Untranslatable, says the Czech writer Milan Kundera. It's a feeling, he says, that is a synthesis of many other feelings: grief, sympathy, remorse, and an indefinable longing. "As for the meaning of this word," he writes, "I have looked in vain in other languages for an equivalent, though I find it difficult to imagine how anyone can understand the human soul without it." In an attempt to explain it, Kundera tells a story. A love story. Boy and girl were swimming in a river. She was a much a stronger swimmer. The boy struggled. He swallowed water. He lagged behind. Feeling humbled, feeling despair about himself and his life, he felt *lítost*. Later, as they were walking home through the woods, the boy, still outraged, slapped her face. She began to cry. When the boy saw her tears, he took pity on her, put his arms around her, and his *lítost* faded into thin air.

"That's all I'm interested in," the filmmaker John Cassavetes once said, "—love and the lack of it."

HIGHWAY TO NOWHERE

Can writing help after the fall, in the recovery process? Is writing therapeutic? Can a writer aid an injured people, an ailing city? Can storytelling heal or even save? One thinks of the mythical Persian queen Sheherezade, whose storytelling not only kept her alive night after night, but also seduced and enamored and healed a wounded king. One also thinks, however, of Theodor Adorno, the German philosopher, sociologist, musicologist, who said that writing poetry after Auschwitz was barbaric. Why poetry, then? Why literature? Why art? Can art flourish only in and around beauty? Or can it—should it—grow out of despair and brutality? *Can* there be poetry after Auschwitz? Or *must* there be poetry after Auschwitz? If writing has no purpose, then why write? If, on the other hand, we accept the notion that writing does have a purpose, or that it can have a purpose, then doesn't literature — art in general—run the risk of becoming utilitarian?

I posed this quandary to two Baltimorese, or Bawlmorese, or Bawlmers, or Ballmers—that is, people from Baltimore.

First, Charlie Duff, one of Baltimore's true authorities on the city's architectural history and development. We were standing on the corner of one of West Baltimore's derelict and eerily abandoned blocks, drinking tepid coffee from flimsy cardboard cups, and looking over a mile-long strip of deserted highway. Highway to Nowhere, it's called. I said that perhaps this was exactly what writing was: a bulky, abandoned thoroughfare that went from nowhere to nowhere. He stared at me oddly. I told him, as I lit a cigarette, that I was a fiction writer, a story writer. I told him that Jorge Luis Borges, the great Argentinean writer, thought that literature was essentially useless. Charlie Duff, smiling in the brisk Baltimore air, took a sip of his coffee, looked at the strange concrete highway, and quoted Oscar Wilde: "The good ended happily, and the bad unhappily. That is what fiction means."

A few days later, we met David Simon, former police reporter for *The Baltimore Sun,* and writer and director of the widely acclaimed television series on the woes of Baltimore, *The Wire.* Had his writing changed anything in Baltimore? Had his writing helped any? He scoffed. "Oh, of course not. Come on. Stop."

MY FEETS IS TIRED

I know this isn't a travel log, or that it isn't supposed to be. But anything you write of your travels becomes just that, a kind of fragmented diary of the places you visit and the people you meet. Thinking comes later. Reflection comes later. If at all. Meanwhile you just travel while trying to keep your eyes open, your step firm and your coffee warmer than your clichés. You go to the battlefields of Gettysburg, and everything there—the trees, the monuments, the crowds of tourists, the t-shirt shops and ghost tours—makes you feel like a cynic. You've been there before. Perhaps on a high school field trip. Perhaps with your parents. Perhaps through history books. You've already seen those fields and monuments. You've already heard the stories of Lee, and Meade, and Pickett's Charge. But now, suddenly, through the smoke and noise of a theme park, you sense it. There it is. You can't yet name it, but you know it's there, and you decide to hide it away somewhere so you won't have to sense it too much, or talk about it, or even think about it, and you drive down to Baltimore. You also know about Baltimore. You've been to Baltimore before. You start walking through the streets of West Baltimore. You see all the boarded-up houses: blocks and blocks of abandoned houses. You take a few snapshots. There's no one there. You think of dead bodies decomposing. And there it is again. Unavoidable. Unmistakable. Now you have to see it. You have to write it down in your travel log. You have no choice. It's too large, too ominous, too important. Why don't you go ahead and write it, then? Why don't you say it? And as you're jotting all this down in your travel log, you can't help but think back to that elderly woman in Alabama who refused to go to the back of the bus. "My feets is tired," she said, "but my soul is at rest."

AFTER FIVE

I first witnessed social upheaval and recovery when I was five years old. A huge earthquake, in a matter of a few early-morning minutes, had destroyed parts of Guatemala City. Whole sections of my city—of my world—had ceased to exist, entire districts and boroughs had been immediately leveled. I now know that more than thirty thousand people died, most while they slept. I now know the history of it: the numbers and figures of what happened that tragic day, in February of 1976, and its consequences. But what I knew then, what I saw and experienced with my five-year-old immediacy and innocence, was closer to the real knowledge. I can still recall, if I concentrate, the smoky and stale smell of the chaos downtown, the dead silence in the birdless trees, the empty stare of all the people wandering about, injured and suddenly homeless. I remember the legions of volunteers, those unsung and unexpected heroes, handing out water, food, clothes, what need be. And I remember all the stories people told. I can write—I have written— from that very place in my remembrance, where literature dwells. For a writer writes of what he has seen, of what he has heard, of the smells and sounds that linger like black moths in his memory. I know from my own writing, and also from that first childhood experience, that a vital part of a people's recovery process takes place through narrative. The stories they tell. The anecdotes and testimonials that, in their telling, seem to mend wounds. Not necessarily in their writing. But in their telling.

I'd read about New Orleans. I'd seen on television the flooding, the bodies, the mayhem, the rooftops sticking out of the water like strange boats. I knew, or thought I knew, what happened in August of 2005. The numbers and figures and politics of it. But as soon as we arrived, in April 2011, the narrative changed, or grew, or somehow became more intimate.

A young taxi driver told me about the red graffiti symbols painted on all the houses after they'd been searched by rescue crews. "They's biblical," he said, and it took me a few minutes to understand that he was referring to the doorposts painted with lamb's blood, in Exodus. A woman in a used book store on Chartres Street told me about wandering around the city with her children. I asked her, perhaps too indiscreetly, about Masperos. She smirked. "You mean the sandwich place up the street, Masperos?" she asked me. I told her I wanted to see their sign. I told her I had heard that, until they changed it, no more than ten years ago, that sign used to say Masperos Slave Exchange— one of the two major slave exchanges in the United States. She just smiled a wry smile. And during an entire morning, in a Loyola University classroom, the writer John Biguenet talked about his friends. He told of a group of neighborhood friends that, every Sunday for two and a half years, still disoriented, would make their coffee at home and then go stand in the street in front of what used to be their neighborhood coffee shop, now destroyed. "Every Sunday, we did this," he said again, "for two and half years, until the coffee shop finally opened." He told of a friend who was forced to move away from her beloved New Orleans, to Texas. "Darling," she said to him, "when I die, I'm not going to know anyone in that graveyard." He told of another friend, a doctor, in dire need of help during the flood, approaching some FEMA personnel in a huge boat, who proceeded to inform him, as they looked at their watches, that it was already after five o'clock and they weren't authorized for overtime, and went back to their hotel. Here, Biguenet's voice suddenly cracked. His jaw trembled a bit. His face turned flush red. He stopped for a few seconds to regain his composure. Almost six years later, I thought, looking away, and his wounds were still raw, his frustration still palpable. For me, witnessing that brief but honest reaction in the telling of this story —that caught even him off-guard —was stronger than any image I'd seen on television, or any numbers and figures I'd memorized from print, or all the politics.

As we were walking out of the classroom, Biguenet mentioned the necessity to write about something that has never happened before, about something no one has ever seen.

CRAWFISH

Driving from New Orleans to Lafayette, we mistakenly got off a back-country highway and crossed an old, rusty, one-lane swing bridge. When we wanted to cross back and get on the highway again, an automatic arm suddenly came down in front of us and we had to wait in the car for ten or fifteen minutes. I'd never seen a swing bridge opening before. I sat in silence, looking at the entire structure slowly swing to one side in order to give way to a small fishing boat. I thought about the loveliness of aged things, about chaos and structure, about the way things used to be, and in some places still are. Someone later said that was the first time in decades they had to open that particular bridge.

The next day, a Sunday, we got on a boat and went on a tour of the Atchafalaya Basin. The afternoon was mild, the water calm. We saw two young alligators, some nutrias basking on logs, several eagles perched in their nests. I caught a catfish with a net. I kept trying in vain to visually understand the water management system in the Atchafalaya Basin. I was sitting in the back of the small boat, in front of our guide, a kind elderly gentleman born and raised in southern Louisiana. He talked to me proudly about crawfishing. The one remaining aspect of authentic Cajun life, he called it. The sun was setting and everything seemed serene and I turned and asked him about a patch of large trees out in the distance.

"Oh, that," he said in his strong Cajun accent, his hand on the throttle, "them's nigger killing trees."

He quickly looked away. He revved the engine. It's possible I misheard him. But unlikely.

A JEWISH TEACHER FROM THE BRONX

Two days later, in Birmingham, Alabama, I stepped outside the hotel early in the morning to smoke a cigarette, and noticed the cover page of *The Birmingham Times*. I had to kneel down to make sure I was seeing correctly. Through the murky plastic of the newspaper dispenser, I made out a large color photograph of a black man hanging from a tree.

Of Francisco Goya's series of plate etchings *The Disasters of War*, Susan Sontag wrote: "How to look at, how to read, the unbearable? The problem is how not to avert one's glance. How not to give way to the impulse to stop looking."

I took out some coins and bought a paper and read the piece right there on the street, dumbfounded, the unlit cigarette still in my hand. A supposed suicide, it said. The family of the dead man disagreed, it said. I thought back to the patch of killing trees. I thought back to the perfectly planted trees in Gettysburg. I thought of Billie Holiday's sad voice, her deep and hoarse voice, giving rise to the poem written by Abel Meeropol, a Jewish teacher from the Bronx:

Southern trees bear strange fruit,
Blood on the leaves and blood at the root,
Black body swinging in the Southern breeze,
Strange fruit hanging from the poplar trees.

Pastoral scene of the gallant South,
The bulging eyes and the twisted mouth,
Scent of magnolia sweet and fresh,
And the sudden smell of burning flesh!

Here is a fruit for the crows to pluck,
For the rain to gather, for the wind to suck,
For the sun to rot, for a tree to drop,
Here is a strange and bitter crop.

There's something eerily soothing in those words. Or in listening to Billie Holiday sing them — cry them. Or in just reading them on paper. Or perhaps in realizing that someone — a schoolteacher — somewhere — the Bronx — was moved enough to write them.

Abel Meeropol wrote his poem after seeing a photograph of the 1930 lynching of two black men, Thomas Ship and Abram Smith, in Marion, Indiana. "I wrote 'Strange Fruit'," he later said, "because I hate lynching and I hate injustice and I hate the people who perpetuate it." In that now famous photograph, as the two black men hang from a branch of the same tree, a large white crowd has gathered to watch. A gentleman points at the dead men with his raised index finger. A teen-age girl smiles. Lynchings in the South, as the writer H.L. Mencken put it, replaced "the merry-go-round, the theatre, the symphony orchestra."

I wondered if Abel Meeropol had felt back then, seeing that ghastly photograph, the same emotions I felt now, eighty years later, looking at yet another photograph of yet another black man hanging from yet another tree? What did I feel? What didn't I feel, as I stood on an empty

Birmingham street with the newspaper in my hands, and the image of the New Orleans' slave trade sign still burned in my eyes, and the echo of the Cajun fisherman's ruthless expression still reverberating like a death drum in my head? How to say all that I was feeling? Could everything I was feeling fit into just one word? Or did I need a bigger word, like Kundera's *lítost*? Or did I, like Abel Meeropol, schoolteacher from the Bronx, need a poem to say what I needed to say? A song to sing what I needed to sing? A story to tell what needed telling? Is art the only way? But what, then, happens to the artist fraught with emotions? To the storyteller whose story is heavier than his own imagination? To the one who sings about the unbearable?

The poet Maya Angelou tells of a night in her Los Angeles home, in 1958, when an already frail Billie Holiday—though only 42 years old—sang "Strange Fruit" to her young son, Guy. As she was singing, Guy interrupted her. "What's a pastoral scene, Miss Holiday?" he asked, and she answered him, Angelou remembers, in a scornful voice. "It means when the crackers are killing the niggers. It means when they take a little nigger like you and snatch off his nuts and shove them down his goddam throat. That's what it means. That's what they do. That's a goddam pastoral scene."

THE CAFETERIA

His name was T.R. German, Jr. He was a Korean War veteran. He talked us through the 16th Street Baptist Church, its architecture, its history, the 1963 bombing that killed four young girls. We asked him questions about that bombing, about the racism and segregation and violence in Birmingham, in the South, and he kept giving us gentle answers. "The Lord is good, all the time," he'd say. "A love that forgives," he'd say. "Be kind to one another," he'd say. To help us understand, he kept telling stories. "They's stories," he said, "but they make sense." He showed us the area where that Sunday ("In America," he said, "the most segregated day is Sunday"), they had found the bodies of the four young girls, lying huddled together under the debris. It was now a cafeteria. Not a shrine. Not a memorial. Not a monument. But a cafeteria. I found this poignant and tender, but couldn't say exactly why. In parting, T.R. German, Jr. asked us if one day we decided to write a story about those four girls—Addie Mae Collins, Cynthia Wesley, Carole Robertson, and Denise McNair—to please write down their names. "Is all I ask," he ended.

As I walked out of the church into the empty Birmingham street, feeling sad but also somehow strangely at peace, I remembered something John Keats had written in a letter. "I am certain of nothing," Keats wrote, "but the holiness of the Heart's affections and the truth of Imagination." [3]

---

3   I take the Milan Kundera quotes from his *The Book of Laughter and Forgetting*. The John Cassavetes quote is from *Cassavetes on Cassavetes*, edited by Ray Carney. The Rosa Parks quote is from "Letter from a Birmingham Jail," by Martin Luther King, Jr. The Abel Meeropol and H.L. Mencken quotes are from the book *Strange Fruit*, by David Margolick. Susan Sontag wrote of Goya's etchings in the book *Transforming Visions*, published by The Art Institute of Chicago. Maya Angelou is quoted from her book *The Heart of a Woman*.

BILLY KAHORA

The Rig, the Church, and the Swamp: God, Life, and Work in Southern Louisiana

"...It's nice work. It's meaningful. It's rewarding.
I don't mean in money terms. It's decent, not like this –"
– David Lodge

"The business of America is business."
– Calvin Coolidge

MR. CHARLIE, OIL RIG, MORGAN CITY

Mr. Charlie, once a busy oil rig, is now a silent giant shed on metallic stilts, his active energy dissipated. He only speaks through his minder Mr. Bob's gravelly voice, when one goes on The Tour. The Morgan City Oil Rig Tour. Mr. Charlie perches on the shore of the Atchafalaya River, eighteen kilometres from the Gulf of Mexico, in Morgan City, Louisiana. He was the first of the mobile immersible oil rigs on that stretch of river, a technology developed in the 1950s.

A new generation of consumer looking at Mr. Charlie saw that it must have been cheaper to leave him here and commercialize him and his history than to tow him away. That seems to be the American way. So Mr. Charlie becomes another tourist attraction, not a Civil War battlefield, nor the site of America's race wars, nor the tourist kitsch of Graceland, but a key cog in one of America's most important contemporary preoccupations: oil.

Mr. Charlie pushes weakly into the low sky, intrusive above the flat floodplains of southern Louisiana. Mr. Charlie's real business remains invisible: the downward thrust of his giant drill into the riverbed of the Atchafalaya. Industrialization has always invited phallic interpretations, and on the tour Mr. Charlie leaves little to the imagination. Beyond the Freudian, Mr. Charlie is a mechanical giant, all arms and floaters, an old Transformer Autobot, long retired. Newer, bigger machines, like the one that caused the 2010 BP oil spill on the Deepwater Horizon drilling rig have taken over the offshore oil industry in southern Louisiana.

We all arrive at the first landing and Mr. Bob says again: "This here is Mr. Charlie." Some of the old men wearing U.S. Army caps "hmmm" and "um" in appreciation at all the gadgetry.

A report prepared by the federal Minerals Management Service and Louisiana State University's Center for Energy Studies outlining the history of oil and gas production in the southern Louisiana area describes the operations as causing a "hostile environment" among the local population. The report offers a colorful narrative with a huge cast of characters, including innovators and pioneers, fabricators, port officials, helicopter pilots and catering crews, divers, truckers, suppliers, boat captains, and able-bodied seamen. Coastal Louisiana, once largely a marsh with the old plantations as hinterland, went through the hyper oil growth of Texas in the 1950s. And Mr. Charlie and the many similar, then new, mobile immersible oil rigs were at the center of it all, staffed by men like Mr. Bob. Like the levees that broke in New Orleans after Hurricane Katrina, Mr. Charlie was built by the military—though not by Army Corps, but rather by Naval Engineering. The first men hired for offshore drilling were experienced in working on and in water, most of them Navy returnees from World War II.

Today, the rigs go out much farther into the Gulf and here on the river, even in the humid spring silence, the heavy machinery suggests industrial noise of a time gone. There is no longer the reek of grease; the sluggish Atchafalaya River below wafts through Mr. Charlie's steel legs, emitting a crawfishy smell. It is early April, and the river is at its highest. Once we clamber to Mr. Charlie's uppermost structures, we feel part of the tower. Mr. Charlie is old, but not ancient enough to acquire the studied preservation of a museum—he just feels abandoned. It is as if all the men—and one can taste the hot grimy work that was carried out here—left one night on their furlough and just never came back.

Mr. Bob starts his lecture: "This here is an offshore rig built on a wooden platform. It is built on a barge in seventeen feet of water." He points out some stretch of land ahead of us called Baton Island, an intercoast between land and the gulf. What we've seen of southern Louisiana, starting from New Orleans, is just streaks of water with strips of land in between. This particular piece of geographical information has little significance, like most of the workings of Mr. Charlie. We are here to understand why the BP Horizon oil spill happened.

Below, Mr. Bob points out all sorts of activities from our vantage point. There is some kind of yard with hundreds and hundreds of sacks of some kind of sand. These are the side products from oil drilling. Louisiana crude is dredged up with a special mud called batonite, which is used as a specialized building material. Mr. Bob fills in the gaps that we sense on the abandoned Mr. Charlie, telling us of the drillers, deckhands and medics who worked it, explaining the mechanics as we follow and aimlessly enjoy the view.

We stop and stand over what looks like a giant metallic sink stopper. His voice shifts in tone. He points to the object and tells us it is called a blowout preventer. So far, we have settled into the rhythm of Mr. Bob's mechanical voice, a working manual of Mr. Charlie's ways. Our footsteps clang everywhere following his voice. Now, one of the old men loudly whispers that it was the failure of the "blowout preventer" that made the BP oil spill happen. Everyone perks up. We are at ground zero—this, the failure of the mechanical stopper, was the cause.

My own ideas about the extraction of fresh crude come from films like *There Will Be Blood,* or the blood-orange flares from CNN Gulf War footage. Looking at the blowout preventer, I picture the thick crude oozing into the aquamarine waters of the Gulf. There are many questions from the mixed crowd on the BP spill, even as Mr. Bob tries to move on.

The spill comes up again and again as we enter Mr. Charlie's entrails, where we walk on greasy dirt. Drill bits that look like alien mouths with interlocking teeth, metallic ropes, machine parts, long and short rods all in various degrees of browning rust. Mr. Bob picks up huge metal stumps with the alien mouth at one end: the key aspect to the oil rig—drill bits. The bits come in different sizes, and Mr. Bob describes them lovingly, all the possibilities of what they can do. We leave them lying there; no one ventures to touch them, treating them as they might a museum artifact or a baby giraffe. Everybody with a camera takes photos of the blowout preventer.

When we come to the long middle mast, it is clear from its size and centrality that this is the heart of the oil operation. This is the long vertical structure that does the thrusting. We look up and down and I imagine that this single contraption is the core of what runs America. Even Mr. Bob's voice perks up.

Next, we come to the living quarters, small cabins with four double-decker beds. This is just like a naval ship, says one of the old men sporting a U.S. Army cap. The living, dining and recreational facilities have a spotless austerity, striking after all we've walked through. The signs get progressively more authoritarian: their exhortations are no longer mechanical but religious. The clean pots and pans, and the sparkling surfaces in the kitchen, are pious in contrast to the hot and dirty mechanical ecosystem outside, warring against the bayou. Mr. Bob's voice becomes less functional, tonally graver—one can feel his regard of it all, the clean, steely, military-like order where he once looked over men playing pool, foosball, watching TV and VCR, playing cards and dominoes. Mr. Bob explains that the workers came in from surrounding states, mostly Texas, took shifts of fourteen to eighteen days, then went to their homes and families for a week with wages in hand. It sounds like good solid work, paying way above the minimum wage. And more, because of the dangerous stuff.

A Gideon's Bible, then something between a technical manual and an inspirational tract for oil rig men, and an evangelical Bible, are displayed prominently on a glass table. The tract is titled *God's Word for the Oil Patch: Fuel for the Soul,* and is produced by the Oilfield Christian Fellowship. A quick flip of the pages reveals that it might not be enough to have military and engineering dictums to run a Mr. Charlie—those are not enough to explain the right of man over nature, over the bayou, the Atchafalaya River, the Gulf of Mexico, or the ocean floor. God is possibly where Mr. Bob's real authority came from. And so the military training, the engineering school, the dictums of modern management, just grease Mr. Charlie's wheels and gears.

Mr. Bob brings up once again the issue of the BP oil spill—abruptly, as if he'd been thinking about it all along and planning an answer to the whole slew of questions that came up a while back. Then he responds, somewhat curtly. He stops—clearly the tour is almost over—and simply says: "It was about somebody not doing their job. Not inspecting the equipment." Mr. Bob, whose last job on the rigs was that of an inspector, pauses, as if he's standing alone.

Before we come down, we come upon a plastic prosthetic arm lying on a shelf just about where we started the tour. It is bright pink, the color of a Jane doll. If everything is in the past, old and gone—the plastic arm seems absurdly normal, a sign of the now reassuringly rust-free rig. After a prolonged silence, with hardly anyone listening to Mr. Bob's summary of Louisiana's offshore oil industry, somebody asks about the arm; he stops mid-thought and looks at us blankly. We gaze at the prosthetic. He shrugs it off, his mind still clearly on the BP matter.

We clamber down silently and I remember Baltimore, the last city that we have visited. And with the postindustrial ruin that is inner city Baltimore, I imagine a time in the future, another rust belt of these wiry structures—not the empty warehouses and parking lots that plague postindustrial America, but hundreds of derricks, in a future of electricity and nuclear energy, when the oft-repeated warning of a time of depleted oil and gas reserves has been fulfilled. For now, the party is still going on. Large oil reserves have just been discovered in North Dakota.

So this is still part of a shiny new world, its embrace is an All-American one of prosperity and jobs; when on Mr. Charlie, the oil spill seems a blip, mere human error. There is an all-conquering purpose to what Mr. Charlie represents. Here, right at the heart of it, it is about good old-fashioned prosperity, low gas prices, the perpetual hunt for energy to subsidize large lifestyles. This is about work that pays, and it is great.

Louisiana ranks fourth in petroleum production and is home to about two percent of total U.S. petroleum reserves. One-third of the oil produced in the United States comes from offshore, and eighty percent of offshore production comes from deep water off Louisiana. The oil industry employs about 58,000 Louisiana residents, and has created another 260,000 oil-related jobs, accounting for about seventeen percent of all Louisiana jobs. The average annual oil-industry salary is $95,000. But at times, there is a stain on the very core of human responsibility when something like the BP oil spill happens. Even military-style conduct and good old Christian values on outfits like Mr. Charlie, or Mr. Bob's curt explanation, do little to help.

BIBLE TRINITY CHURCH, LAFAYETTE

Driving through southern Louisiana, from Lafayette to Morgan City, unless you use the back roads, the freeways flatten the brain, one's thoughts. The giant plains have strip malls plunked on them. Giant trucks whistle past McDonalds, Texaco gas stations, Waffle Houses. Motels and small banks look interchangeable, like modern cottages, then a freeway overpass, then more of the same ubiquitous structures. Closer to the Gulf of Mexico, near where the Atchafalaya River becomes basin, the land is lower than the river, and the levees come up. The back roads are quieter, there is a mulchy feel to the air. If you wander off the road into the fields, the land gradually becomes swamp, more water than terra firma. Children play in yards, there is always a basketball rim, a discarded ball, a man fixing something, a woman with a trowel in hand, all ready with an upward glance, a wave. It is quiet—the interstate trucks don't come this way. When the river behaves itself, this is a good life. Far away from the bustle but with the advantages that petroleum exploitation brings from the high-energy consumption of the oil rig city.

The Sunday morning after our rig tour we head to the Bible Trinity Church in Lafayette, several kilometers away. The church is off the freeway, a technicolor anomaly in a plain frame. There is a rigid assurance to it. Dark brown in the constant greenery, broad and squat in the flat. More concert or film hall, without the usual pretensions of a church space. It is abuzz outside, a small town convention. There are people with wide smiles handing out questionnaires, an intro to the sermon.

If there was a roustabout, working class aspect to the oil rig Mr. Charlie, this feels like the white collar end to Morgan City's oil prosperity, nearer to the $95,000-a-year end. There are about three hundred people in the church. Inside, the room is low-ceilinged, not unlike a posh convention center, somber, windows shut out by royal blue curtains. The sound-track of *Mission Impossible* blares, fitting for the beginnings of this year's Louisiana bright spring. We enter the church in time for the track's accompaniment, a photo-slide that shows the church's efforts with victims of Katrina.

There is a feverish feeling here, as if pious belief has taken the form of under-breath mutters, songs or bible verse. The slide show suggests that salvation here is one of works rather than of faith. A band lounges on the stage. There are photos of baptism rites, and others of barbecue pits. Then a theological video comes on, followed with an excerpt from a Jack Black spoof on Catholicism and wrestling. Then, a rollicking blare from the speakers: "God is Good!" uplifts the building.

When the pastor eventually starts his sermon, he stands before the crowd and shouts: "Why Me? Why Him? Why The Cross?" He follows with several catchphrases: Let us spread the aroma of Christ. Let us "shift gears." Hands stretch out to the ceiling in common supplication. The dress code is smart casual, with the pretense of everyone coming from a bright shiny nuclear family.

The pastor works every earnest pause to build up to a punch-line— Stephen Colbert-Jon Stewart-style in southern Louisiana. The issues are worldly, the Iraq War, the War On Terror, juxtaposed against examples from the Old Testament, with martial metaphors for contemporary life-purpose and work. Joshua, God's "greatest general," keeps on coming up to explain the "transition" America is going through. The pastor yells that toothpaste cannot reenter the tube, and the crowd agrees, with laughter. The general thesis—the Canaanites were superior to all those wild tribes out there that Joshua had to take on. And oh yes, "The buck stops with Joshua." Mark Twain comes up—"Only wet babies like change." Then the pastor throws in that staple of American wisdom, Benjamin Franklin. We are brought back to the near-present through Gladys Knight and the Pips. This feels like it's building up to what America is often accused of, its view of itself as an exceptional nation. But the thesis is lightened by the style, the sermon is aw-shucks self-depreciative, late-night religious commentary on the social and the political. Old Testament meets Comedy Central.

We meet the church leaders after the service. They show us around the church compound and when we finally sit down, the standup effect, the sense of the public performance, is gone. There are two men and two women; one, the husband to Pastor Mary, the leader of the church, remains silent through our conversation. Pastor Mary, Senior Pastor Dennis and a female church volunteer, who we learn comes from Texas, take our questions. It is a calm Sunday lunch-time, and it feels as if we are now sitting with professionals. Pastor Mary is a slight woman with dark hair and a nervous manner. Her earlier genial confidence in front of her congregation has disappeared. She tells us that the Bible Trinity Church was started by the descendants of "a group of rebels" who started the movement in 1981. As she speaks, she keeps pulling her short skirt to cover her bony knees. "They were people who just kind of wanted to follow Jesus, and I don't want to say this in a way that is critical to any other churches honestly coz we've got a ton of amazing churches right here. But in a way it's different from what we do here. It was probably that people wanted to be a little bit more passionate and give their whole lives to a loving God," she says. They wanted to spread the aroma of Christ, she adds. We learn that the Bible Trinity Church began as a small cell in somebody's home, got bigger, and moved to an apartment building party room. The first members then for a long time rented a public school, but as they grew bigger and had to put their babies on the floor and move desks around, they eventually built the building behind us. Since then, some rules have held within the church. Thirty per cent of all proceedings go out to global and local initiatives. And because the church's congregation works in the oil industry, and has grown with time, this is not insubstan-tial. Guatemala, Liberia and Kibera in Nairobi, Kenya, have all benefited from the present largesse of the Bible Trinity Church and, by extension, of the American oil and gas industry. Just as Mr. Charlie brings workers from other oil states of Texas, Alabama, Mississippi, some of the con-gregation travels from thirty to fifty miles away. Bible Trinity Church is effectively a congregation of around one thousand people—an out-sider because it is not part of older Southern plantation gentry, or the fiercely Catholic Cajuns, who live largely apart from the day-to-day workings of oil and gas in this part of southern Louisiana.

Pastor Mary explains the church's worldview through what she describes as humanity's stewardship over nature and the rest of the world. She quotes the book of Genesis, in which God gives humans dominion over earth and all its animals. This, she affirms, is a big responsibility. And that when anything bad happens—this is said in the context of the BP oil spill—man should raise his stewardship of the earth, and that should trump pride, greed and materialism. Pastor Mary also makes it clear that jobs and industry are just as important, and that we must seek a balance between the two. One of us quotes a report that claims that the BP oil spill did not result in any real censure of offshore drilling; the church staffers remain noncommittal on this. Jobs are king in southern Louisiana, even within the confines of the Bible Trinity Church. We also learn from the pastors that small government is good. And that it should not be involved in the communal work of the ministry. However, the Bible Trinity Church is also close to systems of local power— the sheriff, the mayor and local business all come to the church.

Pastor Mary's colleague, the Texan woman with an unruly shock of blonde hair like the lead singer from 80s band Duran Duran, senses our misanthropic pessimism, the possibility that man and his institutions are incapable of restraint. And of course, we keep on bringing up the oil spill. She observes that this is part of the general growth of irresponsibility in the world. Mr. Bob, on Mr. Charlie, saw the failings of a blowout preventer as a failure of systems, and this is not too different a take, albeit a theological as opposed to a managerial one. Senior Pastor Dennis, who preached earlier, does allow that the industry might be pushing natural resources beyond a responsible stretch, then dutifully reverts to theology and says that all must remember their obligation of servitude, which should bring with it a sense of responsibility. The rest nod in agreement when he says that the real failure came from personal irresponsibility, adding that the equipment "worked effectively."

We leave somewhat unsatisfied. We seem in agreement that the real issue at hand is whether one can truly believe in the idea of man's manifest destiny, the strength of self. That is, man cannot be trusted in circumstances where so much is at stake beyond profit. That possibly the idea of self, individuality, and the inherent goodness of man is a false premise, and that the only thing that can prevent oil spills, or inhuman encroachment on bayou lands, are extremely strict legal barriers. But this of course might limit jobs, prosperity, American ideas of "independence." We discuss this later and agree that when our group spelled this out in several ways, there was an impasse with the church leaders. We listened to more theology and felt that the prosperity in the area, brought by the excesses of the oil industry, was hard to overcome, even with the word of God. Both the explanations from Mr. Charlie and from the Bible Trinity Church on the matter of the BP oil spill seem to be panaceas that justify the industry's actions, helping some people sleep better at night. So there is talk of "responsibility," or "self," and a non-interfering government. We have been told about stewardship of the earth. Dominion over all things on earth by man. But Man "fails," equipment "fails." The other reality for both parties was that "we all work for the oil companies and without them the Gulf Coast would not survive."

While still at the church, one of my fellow writers asks the blonde volunteer why the catastrophe befell the residents of New Orleans. "That happens" she says, "to people who put their faith in institutions other than God." Both her and Mr. Charlie's prosperity evangelism have a militant air, not too different from America's bigger, imperialist and macro-economic agendas. And so far Morgan City and Lafayette seem to have prosperous communities from the oil rigs, even while being sheltered in a church that provides different ways of avoiding responsibility for the things they benefit from. Here the oil rig is the secular, and the church the spiritual and evangelical arm of the oil and gas economy.

THE SWAMP

"Late capitalism" said Robyn, nodding.
"What's late about it?"

"I mean that's the era we are living in, the era of late capitalism... big multinationals rule the world."

"Don't you believe it," said Wilcox. "There will always be small companies."

"A few of them will do it, and then after a few years, they'll sell out, and the whole process starts again. It's the cycle of commerce," he said rather grandiloquently. "Like the cycle of seasons."
                                    – David Lodge, *Nice Work*

My first encounter with Louisiana was through Robert Penn Warren's *All the King's Men,* a book loosely based on a place that smells, talks, and feels like what I have seen over the last two days. I first read the book in journalism grad school and immediately projected the imaginary American state in the South — considered to be Louisiana by most commentators — on the political state of Kenya in the 1990s. Penn's dictator-protagonist Willie Stark, a country lawyer bumpkin turned demagogue, was impressionably similar to the Kenyan despot Daniel Arap Moi. Indeed Stark became for me a signifier for the generic corrupt African politician. Jack Burden, the narrator, a historian and journalist turned political fixer, man of rumination and angst, was what I wanted to grow up to be. I underlined almost everything he and Stark did and said, thinking them the wisest things on the nature of politics and corruption, truisms that applied directly to Kenya. "Man is born in sin and dies in sin..." from the Book of Romans, became a favorite.

The big families of the novel, the Burdens and the Stantons, plantation aristocrats whose wealth was built on a post-Civil War quasi-slave economy, were directly comparable to the ruling clan-families in my country: the pre-independence Delameres, then the post-independence Kenyattas, followed by the post-post-independence Mois. *All the King's Men* was a lyrical epic with stretches of folksy rusticity that could have been borrowed from the political rallies of my country. Above all, it captured more than anything I'd read up to that point the rough and tumble ways of politics. And so, while we are heading to the bayou to get a sense of how the Cajun live, I have been looking for signs of Burden's Landing, the land of Willie Stark and Governor, for Huey "Kingfish" Long's Louisiana in Lafayette and Morgan City.

So far the Louisiana visit had been more an exercise in its day-to-day cultures than a dip into its political geography. That was about to change. Before we got here, John Biguenet, New Orleans writer and our host, echoed Penn Warren's book, saying that in this part of America the most important "unit" in politics and business is "the family." That what is known as the old boy network in this part of America consists of extended families that help each out and conduct business.

Louisiana, we've been told severally by different guides, is shaped like an old wrinkled boot, with one or two toes sticking out—the bottomed out L of the state is "Cajun" (as distorted from "Acadia," a French-speaking region in Canada) and in many respects non-American. We have been on the road long enough to start wondering about a bird's eye-view of the land we are traversing, for this lower part is fast disappearing from erosion. In a few hundred years, Louisiana will become rectangular—the toes of the boot will have sunk into the Gulf of Mexico. Now we head there, to the Cajun swamps, to Louisiana's toes. A place, we have been told, that has too much water, too little land, is too rugged, where crawfish is in every other meal, and where a major flood cancels out American optimism every other year. This is the Atchafalaya Basin, America's biggest swamp. This—not Mr. Charlie or the Bible Trinity Church—is what has been affected most by the recent BP oil spill.

On the first trip out on the water, we fly by boat through creeks on the Gulf of Mexico side of the Atchafalaya levees. There are all sorts of leisure boats out there in these mini-deltas, weekend water enthusiasts splashing about, enjoying the sun, water skiing, partying and drinking. Now and then we come to large buoys with company inscriptions, Texaco mostly. Greg Guirard, our guide, explains that these are markers for leased-out spaces under which oil pipelines flow to land from off-shore rigs and wells. Greg looks like a genial Grizzly Adams. He has a low, kindly, but insistent voice — once a college English teacher, he now has an old professorial air about him even after he "decided to go back to the land," meaning the Cajun lifestyle of living from nature. He wears an old checked shirt and tattered shorts. He is so tanned that his skin is like wrinkled bark. Greg is a prolific writer, and has self-published at least six books, both fiction and nonfiction, on Cajun life. He now explains that the spread of water we motor on has been colonized by Big Oil, with support by the Louisiana state government, for offshore drilling. This has destabilized the crawfish and shrimp laying grounds so the Cajun no longer fish there.

Cajuns are Catholics, unlike the rest of Louisiana, which appears to be mostly a Protestant state. There were no Cajuns at the Bible Trinity Church, and I doubt that Greg went to church at all that morning. There is a folksy outdoors way to these Cajun men that suggests they prefer the open swamp's shrouded skies to the pews of a church. In spite of the complaints during the first boat ride, there is luckily enough bounty for all, at least for now, despite big interests pushing them away by decree, or by what they see as systemic bullying.

And so after seeing the worldly side to the river, we chain up the boats to the trucks, drive over to the other side of the levee, and clamber onto the same three boats and enter the swamp. The boats are metallic vats specially built to thresh the hyacinth growing over the water on the swampy side of the Atchafalaya River. Before they seemed like unwieldy ovens in the afternoon heat, and they remain uncomfortable till we get deeper into the different swamp channels, where the Spanish moss and the damp air have a cooling effect. The world on this side of the river is an apocalyptic postcard, framed by grey drapes of moss from the few remaining cypress trees, cobweb-like, as we weave through innumerable emaciated cypress stumps that stand like dead men watching.

The hyacinth carpet thickens and the vats thresh through like a plough knifing through weeds. If hyacinth is a dreaded menace in the freshwater lakes of East Africa where I come from, here it adds ambience, creates pathways, makes the trip more exciting. In limiting navigation, it also cuts down on the number of amateurs who would otherwise come out here. I am in the boat of Roy Blanchard, the second guide. Roy is well over 60, an irrepressible boyish sort, who explains the world in stories, told in an accent that might be considered strange in any other part of America. The closest I've heard is the South African "Cape Colored" accent. I wait for Roy to complain about the hyacinth, but he just shows off his boating skills when we get caught in the thick weeds. The boat's rotors turn clockwise and anti-clockwise, churn us back and forth, all part of the show. As he lays the hyacinth to waste with his rotors, he tells us he built the particular boat we are in.

We go deeper into the swamp, away from the sea, it gets darker, and a day moon appears. We are approaching the last remaining cypress forest in these parts. Roy goes silent and watchful, less the speedster, now the hunter. Temperatures drop and one expects bats to come swinging through the tree causeways. We slowly approach a lone huge nest not too far from the ground in a half-submerged cypress tree. High in the sky a fish eagle swoops up and down, in and out of the bed of sticks. Roy says, "Isn't that just wonderful." The master of this Atchafalayan water-world, he has taken over the lead from Greg on this side of the river.

We come upon a beaver lodge; the Cajun men smell it even before we see it. Within sight we approach slowly. The trees are much closer here; we are in a narrow watery corridor. "Can you see him?" Roy points. At the end of his finger we make out a huge pile of twigs, branches, dry hyacinth, rearranged somewhat differently to surrounding vegetation. Then we make out the plump furry beast and there is a sudden pungent smell that wafts in our direction. The beaver lifts up its face but hardly moves at the approaching low noise of the boat. Closer, the plump animal is filthy in the greenness, with a large rat-like hump, its flat immobile face giving off none of that rodent's casual menace. Our cameras click away and it does not flee. Nothing really threatens the beaver here, apart from the engineering of the Mississippi and the wanton alligator. Our attention eventually rouses the animal and she slips into the cold water with a plop. The water surface stirs. We breathe out collectively. Roy points at the pile of sticks. "There are beaver babies in there," he says with a chuckle. "Cutest things in the world." He turns the boat and we move on.

Roy talks in anecdotes between sightings of the next swamp phenomenon. He tells of baby nutrias even cuter than baby beavers. He tells us that he once took some baby nutrias home as pets for his wife. We get a full reenactment of baby sounds and fuss, his infectious laughter as soundtrack, half-scared we will tip over in this small vessel. "In two days," he says, "the little nutrias stank so bad she washed them with shampoo. But two days later the smell was back. I have never seen anything so cute that stank so badly," he bellows. And so his wife asked him to return the nutria babies to the swamp when the shampoo refused to work.

Story after story, we hardly notice the immutable swamp go by as we listen to Roy. The trees are closer, the moss thicker and the hyacinth now carpets almost every inch of water. Now that we've seen a beaver, Roy is looking for a nutria, an alligator, fish, and frogs — Atchafalaya's version of the Big 5 on this watery safari. We are generally heading towards what Roy calls the center of the swamp universe, to see the largest and only surviving redwood. Suddenly he shouts out to Greg in Cajun: we have come across a fishing line. Roy hauls up a long concentric pipe of net and wire hoops widening towards the end. Inside there are several fish of different shapes and sizes: one is at least 4 feet, a strange fossil creature called a garfish. One smaller fish is still alive and has somehow made it through to the larger hoops and is struggling to find its way out. Roy grabs it and shouts, catfish, to everybody, holding it like a trophy for all to see. He then throws it into the water. Greg tells us that Cajuns make their own hoop nets.

If Roy is about stories, Greg is about systems; a relativist, a comparative sociologist with the Cajun paradise as his terra firma on which everything rests, impatient with anything that is not simple or straightforward. After we spend time together, he becomes impatient with what he calls our "thesis-like" thinking. He reiterates the BP Horizon oil spill, and what it did to this area. He remembers that we have been to a Cajun restaurant, and explains that even the crayfish in these parts had started tasting of crude oil right after the disaster. During one of Greg's lectures, I catch the twinkle of an impressible schoolboy in Roy's eyes. The latter's own anecdotes and joshing refuse to take all this, beyond the practical side of making a living, too seriously. I am not sure whether this simply comes down to their differences in personality.

We move on, and even if we can't see anything alive, Roy stops and shouts excitedly. He reaches for what looks like a dead wet log and chuckles. He pushes the log with the boat and hides it in some nearby brush. Even the third boatman looks envious at this new catch. Greg explains that dead cypresses are a huge resource for Cajuns, for apparently these old logs make great furniture. We learn that the area we are in was all once cypress forest before, as Greg explains, the timber merchants came from the industrial North after the Civil War and bought land for seventy-five cents an acre. They then proceeded to chop off everything and lug it back North. Now logging is not allowed, unless a tree dies naturally, like the one we've come across. We are learning that nothing in the swamp is considered waste by the Cajun community. Greg adds that Cajuns make their own furniture, and that every Cajun is a good carpenter. Even the moss used to be used for bedding and cushions. But synthetic products and efficient production, Greg adds, have driven prices of natural products down.

We've been on the water for almost two hours and we are all starting to flag. The sheer physical spectacle of the swamp, the airy moss hanging above, the hyacinth carpet, the damp air, the confined quarters, the fishy smell, wear thin. We see a baby alligator and Roy tells us that the mother must be close by. As we go deeper, there is more to see. We see a water snake, frogs whose legs are a Cajun delicacy. Roy says he comes out at night with his son to hunt frogs, using lamps to attract the creatures by mass. His stories continue to keep our limited urban attention spans buoyed. When we eventually see a nutria, it doesn't look too different from a beaver, only smaller and darker. Roy tells another story. This time it's about how he'd captured a nutria as a pet and kept it in a shed where all the piping in his home was located. One night he was woken up by his wife complaining that there was a noise somewhere in the house. When he woke up properly he heard squeals. He made his way to the shed and, opening the door, something rushed past him and bowled him over. Then the hot water flew from the shed, scalding him as he lay there. It turned out that the pet nutria had become cold, because it was winter, and gnawed at the hot water pipes trying to get at the heat, bursting the pipes. And so the poor creature was scalded when the water poured out and started complaining furiously at this injustice. Roy is caught up for moments in his own hilarity, even as we exchange some looks between us.

I came to this "indigenous" excursion with some urban suspicion, and even dismissal. A few years ago, I spent several weeks with an "indigenous" community in Kenya, in the Mau Forest complex, the single biggest forest in East and Central African, and an area that impacts at least four countries as a water source. I had been sent there by an environmental magazine to explore the effects of a government eviction of farming communities who had encroached into the forest. There was no question about the legitimacy of the evictions. The forest had been exploited to epic proportions for its timber, for wood for charcoal, for forest glade farming, and a new government had decided to put a stop to it. However, there was a non-farming community called the Ogiek who, at least on paper, claimed to have an indigenous affiliation to the forest. They claimed to have lived off it for centuries, on honey, on a rodent called the hyrax, and since they had not "modernized," they wanted to be the only ones who could remain there. But when we got there, and after some investigation, we discovered some interesting things. As with, many of Kenya's indigenous people who had been absorbed by other larger tribes and their lifestyles, it was really hard to find anyone who was still a "forest" Ogiek. Many had been incorporated into the Kipsigis and their farming ways. Only the old folk, possibly still Ogiek without mixed blood, remembered the old ways and lived on small holdings on the edge of the forest. Also, a new generation had cultivated an economy around being "indigenous," following the wave of donor economies that had sought them out after the huge U.N. Indigenous Peoples' conference in the mid-1990s. There were all sorts of Ogiek community-based organizations that were part of this movement, and which claimed to be retrieving indigenous lifestyles. Furthermore, a few Ogiek elders had been part of a post-independence carving-of-land in the 1960s and so served the political interests looking to stake out land parcels in the forest. Since the Ogiek were on the borders of the forest, their signatures could facilitate the degazetting of common land under law, claiming their community rights to bring the land into private ownership. And this was really the problem with the Mau forest—the people on the edges, the Masai and Ogiek communities had helped farming communities gain access to the forest. Many from these two communities had become wealthy thanks to these economies. The whole "indigenous" cry had become a spin, a ploy to mask what they were doing. And so I found myself questioning the Cajuns' lifestyles and looking for holes in their explanations of how they live. Beyond my encounter with the "indigenous," my questioning of the Cajun lifestyle is also fed by two other reasons. The Louisiana in my head being the state of Warren's Willie Stark, or rather

Huey Long, but also of Kenya, I am looking for corruption everywhere. But after some time with Greg and Roy, I realize that the only thing to question is the idea that they are more conservation-minded than their "enemies," Big Oil. Maybe it is the long boat ride with the never-ending narration of "killing," "taking," "fishing" that makes me wonder whether their lifestyle is just a minuscule appropriation of the environment comparable to that of Big Industry and Big Oil. There is no "indigenous" game going on here, but the Cajuns are self-described friends of the land, and claim their culture to be environmentally friendly.

Writer John McPhee argues in his seminal work on the Mississippi that nowhere else in the United States are there as many competing interests as in southern Louisiana, in the swamplands created by the engineering of the lower Mississippi. And now here one sees that every man is interested in reaping as much off the land as possible. The Cajun relationship with nature is not as Thoreauean as they might think. For starters, what the Cajun hunt is purely arbitrary to circumstance. Crawfish is not, and never was, integral to their "beginnings"; they began hunting crawfish when the Army Corps of Engineers pushed Old River into the Atchafalaya. Before that, they had always lived off the land, not water. But when the engineering of the river took off, and when the Common Water Agreement between the Cajun and other communities and Big Industry was sealed, life and enterprise started working for both groups: the Cajuns lived off the swamp for those months of the year when the waters were released and overflowed, and kept off it bar a much smaller area when the waters were dammed, because the bottomland was off limits while it was dry. So that way, what is dry private land when the water is dammed becomes a common-ownership swamp every five months, during the flood phase of the year. And when the land is dry, the Cajuns can still hunt deer and other wildlife found in the cypress forest but within limits that are much smaller than the wet season when they work the swamp. That way, they can live off the river, albeit in different ways in "wet" and "dry" seasons. They also do this when they come across animals stuck in the marshes. Like offshore oil drilling, their life-style is thus to a degree a result of military engineering. I ask Greg whether the Cajuns would take to the oil rigs if the marine life they depend on in the swamp disappeared. He says that the new generation is already "modernizing." This means Greg and Roy's sons and daughters have started going to college and getting jobs. Even on the oil rigs. In all Greg's books, Cajun "history" seems to have started in the 1950s. There isn't much said about, or before, the beginnings of the five-month flooding cycle. And like the Ogiek, the Cajuns have all sorts of friends to help fight what they see as larger forces. Greg tells us that they have been talking to the Sierra Club and the Audubon Society about how to oppose Big Oil.

We get off the water and head off to Roy Blanchard's house. There are trophy photos everywhere. The lounge is a life-sized album of kill-ing, hunting, and eating. There is deer, some kind of boar, alligator skulls, photos of Roy with some big fish, and with his kids. One photo catches the eye. Roy stands with a string of squirrel skins. I'm still reel-ing from all the swamp bounty we've seen in the Army Corps-engi-neered bumper season — alligators, crawfish, shrimp, catfish, flounder, turtle — and so I ask what the squirrels are for. "We smother them," Roy says with a twinkle in his eye. Why, I ask. You have all that other food. "We smother them with onions," he laughs.

THE PRESENTATION: BEYOND THE SWAMP

Throughout the boat trip, there's been a careful attempt on Greg's part to define the Cajun philosophy, but this really comes through when we attend a presentation he has put together for us the next day. There are several theses to all of it, beyond the swamp. First, there is a strong argument for Cajun simplicity, a kind of thesis of anti-modernity vis-à-vis contemporary American life. Cajuns, Greg reiterates, love life, not money. They also revel in what he calls the simple way of doing things. Once again, he sees our "writerly" questions as too abstract, too academic. Cajuns believe in using their hands. He adds that America has lost its soul because it is so distanced from things it builds itself. Everything Greg explains is juxtaposed against America. If Americans believe that when you are not making money, you are wasting your life, then Cajuns believe that you are wasting your life when you are not having fun, he says. Greg feels that Cajuns have always transcended the racism of the South. And of course, with the groundwork laid, Greg begins a fresh attack on the biggest threat to Cajun culture and lifestyle: Big Oil. This is defined as a clash between the mutually exclusive economies of crawfish, the most representative and profitable of swamp products, and oil. Crawfish are central to the Cajun economy, and offshore drilling and related activities are killing it. Alligators too, moss, catfish—these economies and basics of life have been virtually destroyed by the actions of Big Oil. There has been major commercialization of all activities since the North bought most of the tidelands a hundred and fifty-some years ago, after the Civil War. The idea was to exploit the huge timber forests in the area. He mentions Home Depot and Walmart as significant culprits. The BP oil spill, for Greg, came as the culmination of all this activity.

When the mayor of New Henderson, who is also Cajun, speaks next, he slightly changes the tune and talks of the Big Families of Louisiana. They sound similar to the Burdens and Stantons of Warren's *All the King's Men*. "The big families think they own every elected official. The thing is, you cannot get into the office without their support and once you are in, their demands are in," the mayor says. Greg adds: "We've had these crawfish meetings and we've been unable to get anywhere because Big Business has now taken over crawfish. The prices are so low because there is overproduction."

Greg admits that they see everyone who is not Cajun as "American."

He observes that for generations, and even when he was a young man, Cajuns did not ever marry "Americans," but that has changed. He remembers that whenever it happened, the guy was eventually accepted in the community as a "good guy."

Greg gives us one of his books, and as we flip through it I recognize somebody. The book is titled *Psychotherapy for Cajuns: A Traditional Culture Struggles for Survival in a Crazy World*. There is a section simply titled "Dewey Patin." By all accounts, including Greg's, Patin is a "legend." In the Cajun world this means that he has shot, killed, and wrestled many a creature, on land, river, and even sea. A tale is told of how Patin jumped on the back of a buck deer when he was sixty-five. The previous night, the evening after visiting the oil rig, our group stopped by a restaurant in Breaux Bridge; it had been highly recommended by Greg for its food and music. The place was off the highway, part of a strip mall of activity. This, unlike the oil rig, was the first of many alternative southern Louisiana spaces we visited in our time here. Our first experience of The Cajun World. There were a disproportionate number of brightly colored sports cars and roadsters outside, a yellow Corvette, a red Mustang. The trucks were pretty souped up too, like Roy's and Greg's. But inside there were mostly older couples. Right by the doorway, the Cajun restaurant boasted of celebrity hosts over its long existence —Tommy Lee Jones, Meg Ryan, Matt Damon had all been there. There was a band playing. The three main instruments included an accordion, a guitar and a mouth organ. There were numerous photos on the wall. Flushed smiling faces surrounded tables with heaps of seafood. There was a folksy atmosphere, all the tables faced the dance floor. The lighting was bright. Everyone sat with an easy familiarity, not unlike being in a public family space.

There was an old man on the dance floor. He twirled and twirled to the band whose lead was a twanging accordion. For every other number, the old man got up with his female companion —her long hair invisible, she looked like him from afar, serving that old cliché that two people married long enough start to resemble. The old man's face was expressionless: it was his shoulders and waist that did all the roostering. He danced in turn with three waitresses and with his partner, all night. His chest was puffed out, his thin scrawny arms a twirl. Judging by Greg Guirard's book, the old man is a dead ringer for the Cajun legend Dewey Patin.

Our fare was spare. I asked for alligator, but it was so basted in flour that it seemed indistinguishable from Kentucky-Fried-Chicken. I was still full of boiled crawfish from New Orleans, and alligator was the only worthwhile option at the moment. The frog legs were said to be outstanding but they too came dressed in flour. There was what we soon came to know as standard Louisiana fare: crab, the ubiquitous crawfish, shrimp, alligator, swamp soup, catfish. All these things—the food as we experience it, the dancing man—seemed to have found their way into a simulated narrative: the food into a significant culture and local economy, the dancing man into a legend. No different from anywhere else in the world. But yet, the Cajun region of southern Louisiana is one of mixed fortunes, a lesson in the price communities and individuals pay in choosing an identity other than that of mainstream American. The greatest entity of value and action in America, arguably until Wall Street's recent collapse, is the market, and it demands and reinforces the country's economic, hence cultural, values. Cajun Louisiana illustrates what this value system implies—a lesson about the price a people and a community pay for being different, especially in a place of huge natural resources. And another, learned from Mr. Charlie and at the Bible Trinity Church: the special benefits of staying in line.

Unlike the latter, Greg and his fellow Cajuns see the BP oil spill as the culmination of capitalist greed, of the pervasive disconnect between man and nature. Indeed, he argues, everyone in the area should learn from the Cajuns how to live in harmony with nature. Southern Louisiana also represents the spectrum of different work ethics separating the Cajun and the modern cultures. This realization is not only a local attribute. It is a culmination of the long distance we've travelled on the tour, from Gettysburg, Baltimore and New Orleans to here. In Gettysburg we were told that one of the causes of the war was the perceived difference in relative ideas of work and life between North and South. That in the North, the new immigrants had developed an industrial concept of the use of time crucial to the creation of capital, and that ideas of class evolved through the "proper" use of time for work and application. In the South, the use of time, especially concentrated idleness, lay at the very heart of class privilege, based in turn in family clans. And later we learned that the industrialization of Baltimore was built by successive waves of immigrants, and on the new work ethic of the North. In New Orleans, we were told that the city's uniqueness, and what is described as its "laid-backness," lies in its very resistance to these ideas. Later, John Biguenet pointed to family as the single most important social unit in New Orleans, describing how work and life there revolve around family and historical roots. This can be seen as the opposite of the detached and mobile nature of work in the North, where individuals come and go, pick up work and leave it according to season, with fewer societal and involved relations, and work is not seen as related to any familial structures. In southern Louisiana, the oil rigs have brought in newcomers, similar to work models in the industrial North, while the Cajun lifestyle is familial and societal, and does not separate ideas of work and life.

As I think about the Cajuns and the life they have chosen for themselves in contrast to the rest of Louisiana, and mainstream America, I remember a conversation our group had in New Orleans with David Simon, the creator of *The Wire,* in the wake of our visit to Baltimore. I asked him whether his show, or the work he had done on urban Baltimore communities, had changed anything. He did a double take. "Has anything happened 'cause of my work?" I nodded.

"Oh, of course not. Come on. Stop," he scoffed. Then he turned serious: "The government has been purchased in this country," he started. "We have some very democratic impulses. But they're strained through oligarchic structures. They've now been purchased by capital. You can now buy elections. You can buy whole tracts of government — of the legislative branch. You can ensure compliance in the dominance of capital." He paused and looked across Frenchman's Street where we were, in the midst of all its charm. "And so we're not a republic anymore. We have all the front pieces of a republic but behind the scenes it's money."

David Simon was talking to us on the set of his new show *Treme,* based in New Orleans. What he was saying startled in the midday sounds of jazz, tourists sipping beer, the sizzling of street food. We were surrounded by TV extras looking on, half curiously. A trombone wailed in the background. We had all been overwhelmed by the breadth of this new project, this make-believe world even when we had seen many an amazing American phenomenon. And yet Simon still seemed disillusioned, and it was hard to explain all the work that was being put in there. The tens of extras on set. The several takes that each scene went on for in this new show. The amazing breadth of his novelistic take on Baltimore in *The Wire.* This was a man who had put in a lot for what he had believed in. He went on, and told us that we could write what we wanted. We could explain and make all the arguments we wanted, but that money was the answer to everything in America. The Reagan 1980s came up and how he started the project of converting America's true origins, the labor class, into a middle class, and then into a consumer class. And how this was being dismantled for short-term profits. And so there was now an America for the poor and one for the rich. And then the band played on, inside, to David Simon's words. The Cajuns, I feel, can understand these words.

The night when we fly out of southern Louisiana, a woman in her mid-forties in the seat next to mine peers through her window at the patchwork of land and water below, and asks me what I was doing back there. When I explain, and express a general puzzlement, she smiles and says there is no mystery to the whole thing. She tells me that she has seen many a flood since she was a little girl growing up in Louisiana. She tells me that the key to Louisiana are the three Fs: Friends, Family and Faith. When I think about the Bible Trinity Church folk, and the Cajuns, I realize that these three things hold all of them together, something that might not be true of a large part of modern mobile America. Mr. Bob's faith is linked to a military and engineering order. But what I have also learned is a certain reality to American industry beyond the media, beyond the conspiracy stuff. For standing over the river one also experiences an odd reassurance in the feel of efficiency in the metallic objects, the largeness of the Gulf oil project, the rigs up the coast, the barges, the levees, even the plantation-wide spaces. There is something tangible in these, in spite of David Simon's zero-sum words, for his work recognizes the contradictions and complexities. That even if the enterprise is at bottom-line money, it does not mean that life is totally precluded. And so there is tangibility in the pain and weariness of faces grown old with something extracted from them. This is a far cry from what most see as America, displaced in its smooth corporate corpulence and easy swagger.

Later, at our tour's end, I find myself reading posters in the DC Metro declaring that Natural Gas and Oil employs 7.2 million people, and am now more forgiving of what I had known about the oil industry. Now I can attach to it the faces of Roy and Greg, and Mr. Bob, and their work, and this has tempered many of my knee-jerk assumptions. I now realize that there is more to it, a whole set of intangibles, that many of the "facts" — greed, obscene profits, a certain kind of militant approach — just simplify the story. There is Mr. Charlie and Mr. Bob watching over the river, hoping for better life. There is worship in Lafayette. There is Greg and Roy and their onions that smother swamp life. There is Frenchman's Street and jazz. Even in spite of — and maybe because of — money and work.

KHET MAR

Journey

translated from the Burmese by Tazar

I was born in a small Asian country that is completely different from the United States of America. As a result, my perspective of the U.S. is based on comparative thinking. Spending time in the U.S. has been an emotional shift akin to living in a hut for many years and then venturing into a splendid building and, after beholding its adornments, comfort, luxuries and utilities, seeing the differences between the two sides.

When the initial charm of this splendid building dissipates, nostalgia may occur: one misses the natural breezes of the previous life in a little hut. The deeper I ventured into this metropolitan way of life, the more comparisons I had to ponder. And when I had to consider several American cities instead of America as a whole, the comparative impulse became more complex.

The Writers in Motion traveling program introduced me to various buildings vastly different from the little hut that I came from. But some of these buildings have been damaged by weather and each one has a scar of earlier afflictions. They are nonetheless still much stronger than my native land's little huts, which can withstand natural breezes but are ruined by the country's constant political strife. Besides, these American buildings can still keep something useful from their damage: at least they know how to survive what catastrophes they have endured.

During my early adolescence in Burma, whenever there was an event or a festival in my village, I always hurried to take part in it. When the teenagers of the village showed off in the streets (a traditional way of courtship in Burma's villages and rural areas), I wanted to join them without knowing what it really meant. But as a teenager I was under the control of my mom and grandma; both of them were teachers and strict, disciplined guardians who rarely allowed me to join even regular daily activities like morning exercises or bicycling.

The delta villages were connected by a long, winding common road, or embankment, crossing the back section of each of the villages. Being wider than the others, the embankment crossed our village diagonally. On both sides of this embankment, rice paddies and chili, bean and sunflower fields peppered the landscape. In the rainy seasons, they made a green blanket.

In the winter, the embankment served as a public space and the village's main road. By the time I was a teenager, bicycles had become popular in our village, and in the evenings we kids enjoyed cycling on the road. Mom and grandma weren't bothered whenever I took morning walks, but they didn't allow me to ride my bike every evening. My mom, a silent woman, gave no reason other than saying, "Don't do that." On the other hand, my grandma was very talkative, and spiced her preaching about the do and don'ts for girls with a mixture of her experiences and apocryphal stories.

"This very side of the embankment was a slaughter field once, in the civil war years," she would say. "The Burmese and the Karen tribes brutally killed each other here. At night, people can still hear howls and cries from the side of the road. Your mother was a teenager then. It's a haunted place, and you shouldn't go there after twilight, my dear."

My grandma's prohibition, based on history, was so strong that it chilled me to the bone, and I couldn't find a way to complain about it. Since the road grandma mentioned in her story was located within a stone's throw of our house, I felt faint-hearted alone outside at night. Even during the day, every time I crossed the road with friends, I would check around the side of the embankment, quite frightened. Just the sound of the wind blowing through the trees seemed like a roaring monster. When a farmer shouted at some pesky sparrows in a far-away field, I jumped as if he called my name. The phrase "civil war" stood for fear and an intense negativity for me.

The threatening tone of my mother and grandma's haranguing covered up the actual tragedies of our history, and replaced specific facts with apocryphal tales. Their stories were intended to conceal what they perceived as unlucky history and a jinxed past, and thus to protect us. But they also made me and my generation ignorant of our history, and unable to learn from its mistakes.

When I got to Gettysburg with the Writers in Motion group, I came across the former battlefield area and found it completely different from the forgotten places of my native land. Where I grew up nothing is exhibited from the historical battles; they have been turned into fields of paddy and vegetables and hearsay ghost stories. As far as concrete evidence, once when I was a kid I found a bullet in the field and added it to my grandpa's collection of military paraphernalia, which included a helmet and a tin cup. Our neighbors, too, found something resembling a knife while ploughing the fields. I was curious as to what it really was, and was told it was called a bayonet. I knew by then that soldiers used bayonets to kill people in face-to-face clashes; I was shocked.

By contrast, in Gettysburg there are many forms of evidence and concrete monuments to confirm that this place was once a battlefield. The bronze statues of soldiers, seemingly trying to inspire patriotism, were impressive and meticulously sculpted. On tablets, a variety of exact timelines and the names of generals were provided to the public. The amount of historical information available went far beyond what anyone could absorb in a single visit.

Keeping useful historical facts with a vast amount of references available for public use would be a good example for my native people to follow. At one point, I thought to myself, had there not been a Civil War, or had the so-called Battle of Gettysburg not taken place, what would the town's financial status be? Because of the Civil War and this battlefield's preservation, Gettysburg welcomes millions of visitors annually as a profitable tourist site. When I say that Americans know how to exploit their own misfortunes, I mean it in a good way.

Peter Carmichael, a professor of Civil War studies at Gettysburg College and director of the Civil War Institute, ushered our group onto the battlefield. His eloquence enabled me to imagine the historical episodes, and he gave us detailed information as if he had actually witnessed the battles. The last site we explored was the most dramatic for me. There was woodland on one side of a curved road, and on the other side, a field covered with big rocks.

"This is the most attractive place for me among all other Gettysburg battle sites," Carmichael said. "The soldiers from opposing sides fought to the death in daylight. At night, they kept their guns turned to the ground and gathered here to have a drink. They made themselves forget about the ongoing battle and had a little party. They sang together and exchanged family stories. In fact, they were just searching for their existence as human beings in this place."

The noisy group, chattering and asking questions throughout the battlefield tour, suddenly fell silent. Everyone's expression turned thoughtful. Though I'm not sure about the others, I was considering my own existence.

Burma, my native land, declared its independence in January of 1948. Regrettably, in March 1948, the Burma Communist Party (BCP) went underground. In the delta region where I now live, a coalition of the Karen National Defense Organization (KNDO) and the BCP defended against the strikes of the Burma Army. Since the Karen population made up the ethnic majority in the delta region, both the resident Burmese and the Karen generally referred to these clashes as Karen-Burmese battles. The bitter hatred between the Karen and the Burmese tribes became very common in the country. The Burma Army burned Karen villages and there is no doubt that the Karen also butchered the Burmese whenever they had a chance. To make matters worse, a nation-wide civil war fueled these interracial hatreds. "Burmese" literally means all ethnicities included in Burma (Myanmar), and the Burma Army is com-posed of all Burmese ethnicities (of which there are eight). However, the violence continues today because the very simple and poorly educated local youth mistakenly believe that only Burmese and Karen tribes have killed each other during this time. This young population doesn't real-ize the role the army and parallel groups have played in the killings.

In the chaotic civil war era, rife with many pointless crimes, an upper-class Burmese family from the delta region founded a private army for self-defense purposes. In my opinion, the force was most likely com-posed of extended family and neighbors in the guise of a real army, as is the Burmese tradition. But over time, this armed force became stronger and well-organized, only to be, in the end, hired by the government. The reason the government gave for hiring this force was, needless to say, to subdue regional unrest and to wipe out the rebels. Although the government used the term "rebels," locals understood that this was the label applied to the Karen people.

Ironically, twenty years after the civil war, a Burmese boy who was a descendant of the family-based security force that attacked the Karen people on behalf the government fell in love with a Karen girl who grew up in that same bloodstained spot. They raised their first daughter as a book lover—an interest that prefigured her future career as a writer. That unlikely couple was my parents.

I am perhaps a bit sentimental to say that their romance was like a rare breeze in the long-lasting and agonizing war season. In their con-versations about civil war, I never heard my parents mention bearing a grudge. On the other hand, questions about how to prevent potential racial conflicts and nurture Burma's next generation never seemed to cross their minds; they were simply ignorant in matters of foresight. Such a lack of awareness, common to my parents' generation, delayed the process of rooting out the violent remnants of the civil war that were sporadically continuing in their country.

It is true that we Burmese have failed to make concrete historical records — except for highly subjective texts written by various sides. Unconcern for past tragedies is a nationwide stance. Sharing matter-of-fact historical knowledge is very rare among people, so in Burma there is only a slim chance that a youngster to learn from past events.

Gettysburg is maybe the place that brought the most comparisons to my mind. But the other cities — like Baltimore and New Orleans — inspired questions, as well as a temptation to find more similarities and differences with my home country.

BALTIMORE

Under the sunshine, Baltimore pleased me at first glance. The greenish trees and spring cherries were particularly attractive. The sunlight lured me in and I joined the walking tour to explore the town, wearing only a light sweater.

Unfortunately the breeze, turning colder, was a test of our curiosity about this place, and of my strength to withstand the increasing chill. Baltimorean Charles B. Duff, developer, planner, and authority on Baltimore's architecture, ushered our strolling group around. Duff knows the relevant dates, figures, and events by heart, and his lively conversation accentuated his awareness of and enthusiasm for his native town and community. He also pointed to racial divisions that were a significant part of the city's history. He said: "In 1962, the city bought whole streets of crowded houses and tore them down...Why? To divide the city. This was called a 'firebreak' — a corridor designed to keep the races separated, to stop the 'fire' from spreading. They tried to protect a white neighborhood from a black neighborhood, and it worked."

As my mother belonged to the Karen, my country's minority ethnicity, and my father was part of the Burmese majority, my siblings and I grew up in a Burmese village. Since I was my father's daughter, my appearance swayed towards Burmese. Because of this, my Burmese friends warned me about Karen rebels. In contrast, my mother's kin bitterly gossiped whenever a Karen married a Burmese, chastising that person for polluting Karen blood. Being Burmese, the slogan "beware of Karen" makes sense to some extent, but the pressure to be "pure blood" seemed to be (at that time) plainly Karen nationalism. Still I made certain that my own existence — the fruit of Burmese-Karen parents — didn't bother anyone. As a rule I am not antagonistic, and create no dissension between the two sides. I never hesitate to introduce myself as a Karen, and I am proud to be Burmese.

In America, a country in which slavery and racial inequality resulted in a civil war more than a century ago, there are cities still rife with racial issues. Baltimore seems to be one of them. Once a city with a large population, in the 1980s Baltimore's numbers were in decline. The city's high unemployment rate caused an exodus to the north where factories were running. Since then, Baltimore has been relatively bereft of new growth, with over 15,000 houses standing empty. What will the local people do with these empty houses? What will be the future of this beautiful town? These were my questions.

NEW ORLEANS

I was particularly interested in New Orleans, where I wanted to visit areas ravaged by the infamous Hurricane Katrina. But when I arrived in the city, its surroundings and landscapes evoked the sights and smells of my native Burma: the radiant sunlight, the shady woodlands, the aromatic breezes; the variety of seafood too — the fish, lobsters, and prawns — reminded me of my home in the delta region.

Here we were visiting the set of American producer David Simon, who was filming *Treme,* a fictional television series that depicts life for New Orleans residents following Hurricane Katrina. The *New York Times Magazine* called the series "a sign of the city's inextinguishable joie de vivre," and the street—not far from the well-known French Quarter— was certainly crowded and buzzing with actors, extras and film crew. I was told Simon consulted with New Orleans musicians Donald Harrison, Jr., Kermit Ruffins, and Davis Rogan, as well as local chef Susan Spicer and civil-rights attorney Mary Howell while developing the series. Many of the people hired to play parts in the series and who moved about the crowded set were locals who had experienced Katrina firsthand.

On that bustling set my mind wandered to my native land and people, who never had the opportunity to tell the story of their misfortune, let alone to earn money from it. In May 2008, the cyclone Nargis hit Burma. It was nearly as powerful as Katrina, and a lot more devastating. Nargis left millions of people homeless or dead. But the government suppressed Nargis victims' stories: survivors were not allowed to write or publicly share their firsthand facts or testimonies, let alone have those stories filmed in such a celebratory way. In fact, about thirty rescuers who volunteered to help cyclone victims eventually found themselves behind bars, and half of them are still jailed, now in different prisons.

At the gathering point for the Disaster Bus Tour, there were long queues of people waiting to explore the hurricane sites, as well as parked tour buses full of passengers. I was again reminded of my thoughts at the Gettysburg Battlefield Tour—that Americans can use unlucky events for positive purposes, including making money. In Burma, the work of journalists and writers must pass a strict Literary Censorship Committee. While Americans were able to use Katrina stories to earn money for local people, some Burmese writers weren't able to tell people about the cyclone, and those employed through official channels used risky alternatives—such as blogs or online media—just to inform the public about victims, most of whom could not even afford to rebuild their little huts after Nargis hit.

After touring the areas struck by Katrina, we took a motorboat tour of the Atchafalaya Basin, which reminded me of aquatic experiences that were once a vital part of my life. Since most of my friends were fishermen, I spent childhood days swimming in streams and rolling on the river. From them I learned how to catch fish. As soon as they finished primary education, my friends became professional fishermen. My early published texts were stories about these fishermen and accounts of life in the delta villages. As I visited their huts and listened to their exciting tales, I was, in my mind, rendering their stunning accounts in words.

In a way, my entire childhood and youth in this fishing village was an inadvertent case study of that aquatic lifestyle and atmosphere. The village's well-off fishermen could enjoy their morning meals of fried dried-fish, but the majority of fishermen had to row for a solid two hours just to reach a spot to net, which they did all night long, mostly in rainfall. When they finished, they had to row back home for another two hours. The total amount of fish caught in four hours of rowing and rain-soaked, night-long netting was their family's meal for a day. No matter how heavy the previous day's rain, the worn-out fishermen had to fish every single day to avoid starving. And because the stitched *nypa*-leaf roofs of their skeletal huts generally could not resist heavy rains, sleeplessness was a common enemy.

The majority of the fishing villages on the Atchafalaya River was made up of Cajun tribes — inhabitants coming from France in the eighteenth century. Even today, many of the adult Cajuns speak French. Local fisherman Roy Blanchard, as well as fisherman-writer Greg Guirard, guided us on our exploration of the area, pulling their fishing boats by car. The vicinity of the Atchafalaya River, a branch of its mother the Mississippi, is a delta area with surrounding lakes. Historically, the local people lived by fishing for prawns, lobsters, crawfishes, and even crocodiles.

The delta soil and marine-based economy were more than a source of monetary stability; they were also part of the regional psychology — an atmosphere that was part of their simple-yet-happy lifestyle.

In the preface of Guirard's book *Psychotherapy for Cajuns,* Annie Blanchard, who was born in the Atchafalaya Basin in 1947, said: "If you look back on it, people would call you poor, but we never knew that feeling of being poor. We had everything we needed. Money doesn't make you happy. Money just makes you crazy."

I am pretty sure my fishermen friends and their family members did recognize the taste of poverty, since they, too, were deprived of many vital things. While some Cajun fishermen claim that money doesn't make people happy, they were a lot luckier than my fellow Burmese fishermen who owned extremely age-worn, motor-less boats, which they often rowed while cupping out the water as it leaked in. The father of one of my friends was an elderly fisherman who had fished for survival for many years. He became ill with stomach cancer and wanted, as is traditional for sick people, to eat a bit of rice, dried fish, and spiny eel to help his recovery. Sadly, all the spiny eel and other fish he caught had to be sold for his family's daily needs. He noted the irony of this predicament: "What a life. I cannot afford to buy the eels that I caught all my life. I'd rather die."

Cajuns in the basin region have a great life philosophy, as expressed in Guirard's book. Unlike the more widely held American belief that "If we're not making money, we are wasting time," Cajuns — who are devoted to their identity and customs — have a different and wonderful definition of life: "If we're not having fun, we're wasting our time." In my opinion, only a man who is content with his own existence can feel happiness. I have no doubt that Cajuns are these sorts of people.

For example, Myrtle Bigler was born in Atchafalaya Basin, where she also passed away at the ripe old age of 95 in 1995. Guirard quoted her as saying, "Some people think we are crazy to be living out here on the river by ourselves. I think people that live in cities must be crazy."

Myrtle's words highlight how contented she was with her own humble life. The art of gaining that type of satisfaction requires the ability to value one's own neighborhood. Cajuns love their native soil and value their delta resources, which provide them with numerous foods. They understand that they must maintain their natural resources.

Nonprofit groups like Lower Mississippi Riverkeepers were formed with that awareness in mind: "to educate the public and community leaders about water quality issues on the river; to provide a base for activists to improve river conditions; to monitor and investigate incidents reported by citizens to our toll-free hotline; and to target polluters and compel compliance." These objectives establish a mission to maintain the water quality and flow of the Mississippi River, both for current users and future generations.

Sadly, this perspective is not present in my native delta villages. Since my early childhood, the rivers and streams were places to dump garbage. When I returned in 2008, the delta area of Burma had suffered a great shortage of drinking water, in spite of its impressive appearance on Google Earth, with many rivers that run like veins. I couldn't believe my eyes: the stream that served as a main transportation route and carried many boats and motorboats in earlier days had turned to an unusable, muddy brook. At that moment, my thoughts were running to and fro, like the boats in my deep memory.

In our country, local people, including my fellow fishermen families, did not understand the importance of maintaining the soil they lived on, nor did they know how to do it. They didn't know about well-being because they had no access to education or knowledge, drowning in poverty at the hands of a leader who did not possess even the slightest willingness to improve their conditions. And isn't it true that the fate of a people, more or less, depends on the leader of that country?

Roy said that even the Cajuns, who have much awareness of their identity and customs and have lived on marine products for centuries, now only have a few people still involved in marine life. Nowadays, the older generation takes a break from their other work and comes back to the area to catch crawfish in season, while many local youths flock toward larger cities in search of job opportunities. The modern age has allowed Cajun youths to choose from many more professions, and these options have gradually blurred Cajun traditions and ethnic philosophies.

BIRMINGHAM

"Equal and exact justice to all men
of whatever state or persuasion"
– Thomas Jefferson

I took note of this quote on a wall at the Civil Rights Institute of Birmingham, Alabama. Like my visit to Gettysburg, the evidence of discrimination exhibited at the Civil Rights Institute drew my attention. The forms of discrimination we read about in books can be seen there in pictures, statues and documentary films.

However, at first glance it was hard to believe the city's nicknames — Bad Birmingham and Bombingham — or that it was once known as the most thoroughly segregated city in the United States. In fact, that day was one of the most pleasing days of the trip. The spring sun was very bright and the sky a tranquil blue. Everybody seemed refreshed in the pleasant atmosphere. On the street, African-Americans were chitchatting and having fun. As our group included Asian, African, Canadian, European, Australian and local American writers, its appearance was quite varied. Seeing that we were foreigners, several locals greeted us cheerfully while we paused in a park. They never concealed their curiosity, asking where we were going and what we were planning to do.

In a cozy little café, an African-American woman with a heavy layer of make-up, moving her body to the music, was preparing a coffee for my friend Madeleine. Across the counter, an older African-American man with a friendly look asked if I liked Birmingham. I had recently enjoyed my first chicken gizzards from a take-out restaurant across the street and was quite amused. When I answered, "Of course I like Birmingham," he commented, "It's strange," still smiling. I'm not sure what he meant by this. Maybe he thought I didn't really like the place, or maybe he was commenting on how strangely different Birmingham's present is from its past. Maybe most of the people he meets don't like Birmingham, but I did.

On our first day in Birmingham, we visited the city and its tourist sites with our host, Professor Pamela King. Birmingham was established in 1861, as a post-Civil War city. Between 1876 and 1965, Jim Crow laws were enforced, meaning racial segregation in public schools, on public transportation such as buses or trains, and in public places such as restrooms and drinking fountains. These laws also created Birmingham's segregation zones. Professor King led us through the old Jim Crow district. Most African-Americans from this neighborhood worked in steel manufacturing and coal mines in the early 1900s. The most powerful Communist party in southern U.S. was also established in Birmingham, King said. Today Birmingham has blossomed with many industries and an active civil rights movement.

The American Civil War revealed the empathy of whites and was essentially a victory for blacks — many white lives were sacrificed. In the 1950s, though, there were dozens of bombings by unknown terrorist groups. Usually, the targets were black-owned properties or financial buildings. That is how Birmingham was sadly nicknamed Bombingham. In the 1960s, when it was dangerous for blacks and whites to even walk the streets together, Dr. Martin Luther King, Jr. strove for a second victory for his fellow African-Americans, and his struggles were particularly based in Birmingham. In his "Letter from Birmingham Jail," he famously wrote "I am in Birmingham because injustice is here."

I could see evidence of that injustice in the Civil Rights Institute of

Birmingham, watching examples of schools' and facilities' segregation, buses labeled "White" and "Colored," documents from coal mines in which African-Americans were working at great risk.

Another sentence from King's "Letter from Birmingham Jail" reminds me of the tendency to stand on the sidelines: "Injustice anywhere is a threat to justice everywhere," it says. In my interpretation, to neglect even a little bit of injustice and accept it as commonplace is to threaten justice in general.

Because Dr. King's philosophy of justice sowed the seeds for the advancement of the Civil Rights Movement, African-Americans could reap the fruits of his labor in later years. In 1971, the first African-American mayor of Birmingham was elected, backed by white businessmen.

No one should miss visiting the 16th Street Baptist Church if they have a chance to see it. I was told that this was the very first church in Birmingham built by people of color. During the Civil Rights Movement, whites bombed the church, resulting in the murder of four African-American girls. Our guide, T.R. German, Jr., in his late sixties, explained the background to us at length. In a short sentence from his long talk, I saw a glimmer of hope in the midst of this church's tragic history: "We stand now being able to forgive," he quoted, pointing to a stained-glass window called the Wales Window. The hands of the African-American man in the glass window are in different positions: In Mr. German's interpretation, one hand indicates forgiveness, the other oppression.

On a bulletin board in the church, a piece of paper under the sign "Daily Reminder" made me smile. It said:

Love strong!
Forgive strong!
Believe strong!

Both in Mr. German's words and in the sentences on that wall, forgiving was mentioned over and over again yet it seems that the Civil Rights Movement didn't necessarily base itself in forgiveness. In striving for the rights and equality of blacks, forgiveness alone was never adequate. It is true that forgiveness is a word of virtue in its positive sense, but it is not the cure for all diseases. When a nation, a race, or a group of people do an injustice to another, the victims should meditate on forgiveness for their mental health—the members of the 16th Street church probably had practical experience with the benefits of forgiveness to believe in it so strongly. At the same time, victims should not forget practical means to fairness such as resistance, negotiation and revolt.

At the Arlington National Cemetery in Virginia, a young Asian woman with black hair stood among the colorful tulips backed by the deep blue sky, smiling. Her smile was big enough to almost close her eyes, and looking at the girl and the setting, I experienced a sense of déjà-vu. My mind searched for the exact place and time of that episode. The images became clearer but seemed floating. Finally, I got it. It was not my real past-experience, but an episode from a dream. To feel déjà-vu is rather weird, but I assured myself that memories are just saved in the subconscious part of our brain—I probably visited the sunken part of the iceberg of my consciousness, or maybe it was a spiritual experience.

Though she is currently living in Canada, throughout the trip Madeleine Thien, a daughter of Chinese parents from Hong Kong and Malaysia, made me feel at ease with her huge smile and soft voice. Convinced I had seen her in my dreams, I felt a deepening intimacy between us.

At the very start of the trip, at the Gettysburg battlefield, Adisa Bašić from Sarajevo asked me, "What makes you miss your native country the most?" She could fathom my homesickness, and tried to comfort me. Her laughter gave me a relief from my fatigue and my profound unhappiness. Thanks to Adisa I got a taste of a happy-go-lucky attitude for a while, even though I am typically introverted.

Through my involvement in the International Writing Program, I met its staff members Nataša Ďurovičová and Hugh Ferrer. Our trip started on April 3rd, and just a couple of days later, I heard the sad news that my only younger brother passed away in Burma. Nataša said that she was sorry for my brother and consoled me with a brief hug for my bereavement. On the day when we were supposed to meet with a group of students from a creative nonfiction class for a reading program, I stayed behind at a fried-chicken counter for lunch with Nataša for company. When I apologized for my lateness, Hugh, the director of IWP said, "You're good, you're not late," and hugged my shoulder. Their brief gestures made me feel a huge relief, and created a long-lasting warmth in my heart.

It was Alice Pung, an Australian-born Cambodian girl who knocked on my door after I told Hugh I preferred to stay in my room instead of going to dinner because of back pain. "How do you feel, Khet? Are you okay to be alone at the hotel? Should I stay with you here?" she asked. Again, I felt a profound warmth, and I was certain she had a heart of gold.

During our motorboat trip in the Atchafalaya Basin I saw masses of water hyacinths and *Enhydra Fluctuaus* (called *kanaphol,* or water spinach, in Burmese), which are very common in my homeland. When I mentioned that water spinach was considered an edible plant in Burma, the Jamaican writer Kei Miller's eyes gleamed. "How do you cook it? Which kinds of ingredients do you need? Can you cook it, Khet?" When I said cooking oil, salt, a little chicken powder and garlic were enough to fry it, Kei encouraged me: "We should try it. It's an adventure." Other writers in the boat, too, were ready to help me collect the water spinach. I really regretted I had no chance to make a water spinach curry for my fellows during the trip — but water spinach appeared as an ingredient in one of Kei's poem.

The Philippine Vicente Garcia Groyon and my friend Sarge Lacuesta were old friends, and Vicente would whisper "Southeast Asia..." to remind me we are neighbors, whenever he visited my seat, or I his.

Eduardo Halfón, the second writer-in-residence at the Pittsburgh program where I currently am the third, is a close friend of my neighbor Horacio Castellanos Moya and his wife Silvia Duarte. He never failed to ask about my family and my health. He also never hesitated to express his exact feelings and perspectives when we talked about my nation's political affairs. Usually, my mood lightened after these chats. We visited each other's country in words. Because of his brimming knowledge our group called him "Dad Ed."

Billy Karanja Kahora from Kenya is a friend of my friend Peter, from the University of Iowa's 2007 IWP fall residency. During our lunch hour in a little park in Birmingham, Billy handed me some chicken gizzards and I had a taste. The next day, as other members were enjoying sandwiches, Billy and I walked two blocks for more chicken gizzards. Those steps in the streets, the hours we spent together, eventually appeared in my texts, widening their vanishing point.

In this Writers in Motion program, we writers were supposed to study America, especially its moments of falling and recovering throughout history, to share what we perceived with our readers. We ventured into the perplexing catastrophes and the very slow, gradual process of recovery. We also got a chance to take a step into our fellow writers' subjective worlds where we could share our personal misfortunes with each other in loving-kindness.

Every country's failures are of global concern, and through fellowship with other countries the recovery process can be accelerated. That global fellowship can be attributed to the empathy we felt, I think.

After all, from an alien's point of view we all look like earthlings.

Although we live on the same planet, we also live in very different worlds that are kept apart by native peoples, atmospheres, cultures, and governing systems. It is more difficult to imagine people living in their private worlds as global citizens than it is to access each one's private world by making friends with them. Readers should be able to access the private worlds of the writers on this trip via their different texts.

I visited many houses that were profoundly different from my native little hut. I saw both familiar and strange homes and asked many questions, reasoning comparatively, trying to build mental bridges between these places and my native home. In these two weeks we tried to connect what really happened in these places and the people who survived those events. Given the brevity of our visit, we were to be temporary bridges between communities. But I believe those temporary bridges were meant to be the bases of long-lasting concrete bridges that will serve as paths to a brighter future for the people currently struggling in parts of the world that need to be rebuilt. I cannot decide what the exact definition of a brighter future is; nor can I simply hope for a utopia. What I can say is that through our connections with these places, and with each other, we took part in that endless odyssey toward a brighter future. That joy alone brought us close enough to the purpose of our trip.

KEI MILLER

The Grief Spaces

This was supposed to be a travel essay, and in a way it is. But I imagined (before it had been written) that it was going to be about the actual places we had travelled to. New Orleans and Gettysburg. Morgan City and Lafayette. Perhaps it is testament to my newness in the genre that I should have thought such a naïve thing. As it turns out, this is as much about me as it is about America. And I think it has to be. I think this is always the case with this kind of essay, that it is as much about the journey-goer as it is about the journey, and that the hundreds of miles we travel by planes or by buses do not come close to the thousands of miles we travel on the inside.

Also, this is about my mother who did on this trip what the dead always do so well—she haunted it.

Call it superstition, but I believe I may have summoned my mother to join the trip. It was an accident. I didn't do it on purpose, and I have decided from now on to be careful of the first conversation I have when I arrive in a new place. First conversations have a way of framing everything else. As soon as I had disembarked from the plane, I ended up talking about my mother and, as if invited, she came off the plane right behind me.

It had been a long flight was from Scotland to America. Not as circuitous as it could have been, but long. I flew from Glasgow to Heathrow and then here was a long gap — long enough for me to go into the city and spend the day at Hyde Park. Later I flew from Heathrow to Baltimore and when the plane landed it was already night. There is something about airports in these late hours that reminds me a little too much of hospitals — the large, stark whiteness of it all; the surly janitor vacuuming; the drawn faces of loved ones patiently waiting. I was the last of the writers to arrive. Hugh Ferrer — bless his heart — had waited on me. We got sandwiches and sat down to talk while waiting on the car to take us into Gettysburg. I looked at Hugh and thought to myself, he hasn't changed any! Though in all fairness, it hadn't been that long. He was still tall (which I guess is unchangeable) and still blond and still lanky. The foot-long sandwich he had ordered I knew would be lost without a trace in the vortex of his fast metabolism, while my sandwich would become part of the five or so extra pounds I was resigned to gaining while in America.

Hugh wanted to know what had been happening in the three years since we had seen each other, so I told him about the new books, and about the PhD, and that my mother had died. He said he was sorry. I thanked him because that is what you do when someone offers condolences, you thank them. But when I thought about it, it occurred to me that Hugh was someone with whom I could risk honesty. So I told him something else. I told him it was a strange thing being a writer going through grief — or at least trying to go through grief. I told him that I hadn't been able, even after almost two years, to cry or to be catatonic or to break a plate or to throw a tantrum in a supermarket aisle over the lettuce or to just have a good and proper nervous breakdown. I couldn't do any of it because I was so busy observing myself. I felt self-conscious in the most profound and horrible way. Nothing I did would feel authentic — I would think I was just performing.

I told Hugh how I had gone back to Jamaica for the funeral and found one of my cousins waiting for me at the gate of my parent's house. His arms were opened wide ready to receive my embrace, and his face was creased with pity. He kept on saying, "My God. My God," all the time waiting for me, willing me, to hug him. I hated that moment, and perhaps in that moment I hated him. I resented what my cousin expected of me—that I should perform some kind of public grief so that he could be released into his. I didn't want any part of it—not then. I gave my cousin a sad smile and shrugged. "Yeah, it sucks." I did not return his hug, or wail into his shoulders. I did not release him into the grief he wanted to be released into. My mother was dead, at the age of 62, and all I could say was "Yeah, it sucks."

And that was the first conversation I had when I landed in America. It framed everything else.

Back when I thought this was going to be the kind of travel essay that simply described landscapes and cityscapes and the people that populate them, I had prepared. I took photographs of rusted oil rigs and collapsed roofs and the watermarks high up on the house walls of New Orleans—watermarks that said all too poignantly: people drowned here. I also scribbled down notes, little impressions, small reminders of bigger stories, like a note that simply said—"woman screaming at fallen bottle in Downtown, Baltimore."

The larger story would be this: we had returned to Baltimore from Gettysburg, checking in to the hotel on a day when the sun was shining. Gettysburg had been chilly and so the feeling of spring meant that I wouldn't stay too long in the hotel. I put down my bags and went back out, on my own. After about twenty minutes of wandering, I found myself at the Old Lexington Market.

I had a strange feeling being there. I thought to myself: here is a place where I should be fitting in. Here is a place far, far away from white America, and here I am, a black man with dreadlocks. Most of the people here are also black men with dreadlocks. And maybe that's the reason I felt conspicuous. It was because I thought I should have fit in, but instead I was aware of my not-baggy-enough nor low-enough jeans; aware of my inability to walk with swag; aware of my recently acquired British vocabulary—"Cheers" and "Ta" and the unfortunate habit of using the adverb "rather" rather too often.

I walked from stall to stall trying not to stay so short a time that it would seem impolite, nor so long a time that the vendor would ask, "What do you want?" (I have found that this neither-too-short-nor-too-long time averages about 2.5 to 3 seconds). Eventually I did stop, and at one of the busier stalls. I joined the line for a crab cake, not because I was hungry but because someone somewhere had told me that if there was one thing I ought to eat in Baltimore it was a crab cake.

In the line, I began to focus on the woman standing in front of me. There was something odd about her. She never moved forward unless someone shouted at her to move, and even then it was not until the second or third shout. She was almost catatonic, like someone who had been irreparably damaged by drugs, which I am guessing was the case. She was humming to herself as well, a single undecipherable note, and clutching a brown paper bag. She clutched the bag so tightly that it revealed the shape of its content—a bottle. Occasionally the paper-bag would fall from her hands, and this would surprise her greatly. She would look to the floor and begin shouting—such a wailing as if the paper bag and its bottle were misbehaving children that she had finally tired of. In a slow and lumbering way, she would finally bend to pick up the bottle that thankfully never broke and the process would start all over.

In another airport, less than two weeks after my conversation with Hugh, I would have the same conversation again, and I would be unaware that I was repeating myself. Maybe this is just the nature of haunting, the way of ghosts—they keep on showing up until we have understood them. Mercifully for Hugh, the second staging of this conversation was not with him but with Vicente Garcia Groyon.

Vicente, a novelist from the Philippines, is a quiet man. He has the kind of reserve one might generously call "dignity" and one might well be right. But when I told this very quiet, this possibly dignified man, about my mother's death and my inability to cry, he was incredulous. "But you must!" he insisted at first, but then his writerly self kicked in and he tried to put himself in my shoes. He told me then, "Yes, it was almost the same with me when my grandmother died. I didn't react at first. But then I had to say something at her funeral, and I broke. I cried and I cried, and it was beautiful."

I knew what he meant, and I probably should have told him then that I came to the verge of such a moment. At my mother's funeral, I was asked to say something. I thought if there was one thing I could do for her I could say something beautiful at her funeral. But not just beautiful; it had to be funny. It had to be something very, very funny because that it is how it was with us. Any time of day I thought of a joke I would call my mother and share it, knowing that she would laugh loudly and scandalously. The neighbours would hear her too, and they would hardly believe that this woman in the house next to them was ill and had been in bed for a few years. So I made sure that this thing that I wrote for her funeral was beautiful, but that it also included moments where people could laugh. In fact, I wanted them to laugh so loud that anyone passing the church would not believe that a funeral was happening inside.

On the day of the funeral I read this thing—this very funny thing—and people did laugh. But near the end my voice stumbled as if the thing I was reading wasn't funny at all. My voice stumbled all the way towards breaking and I had to take several breaths before I could continue. I was finally able to but it was too late. Everyone who had been laughing was now crying.

Later that day back at the house while the goat was being curried and the mannish water was being cooked, and while everyone was settling into their hushed little groups, I stood by a tree just watching it all.

An aunt came up to me and said, "It was a beautiful thing that you did today. You made me cry."

I wondered, why should this be a compliment? Why is it good to make people cry? I found it all the more strange coming from her, because this particular aunt had been crying from the moment she came off the plane from Boston and hadn't stopped. I was sure I had nothing to do with her outpourings of grief. But now she was dry-eyed. She took my hand and said again, "It was a beautiful thing that you did. It was an important thing."

I thought of my cousin then, waiting for me at the gate, his arms open, wanting from me a simple gesture — that I should collapse into his arms and allow myself to be weak with grief; that I should hold on to him tightly and allow some kind of broken sound to come out of my mouth; that I should in turn allow a broken sound to come out of his; that we should be caught up in a mutual outpouring of sadness. And I finally got it.

In those moments when grief is lodged inside us, we all look for something to help it out — someone to hold us so tight and squeeze it out from us so that it is no longer a thing in our throats or behind our eyes or in our bellies. The strange thing is this: we don't want grief to be inside us, but we want to be inside of it. We want to enter into a grief space, because then we could do our grieving and leave. And that very funny thing I had written for my mother had become such a grief space. My aunt had entered it, done her grieving, and left.

I began to think of our journey, from the ghettoes of Baltimore to the Cajun communities of Louisiana, as a trek through "Third World America." It sounds like a contradiction. In fact, there were places that we got to that didn't even consider themselves America. They understood that there is a large and pervasive idea of what America is, and they understood that didn't fit into this idea. In New Orleans, we had been told, without any irony, that "when the disaster struck, we just sat there waiting on America to show up and lend us a hand." America clearly was somewhere else.

But all of it was America. The places might not have imagined themselves as belonging, and their belonging was an uneasy one — secured by a civil war that hasn't been completely forgotten. And also, these were not the places we usually imagined as America, but the fact of them — this cluster of peripheral, almost tangential realities — should not have surprised me. For who is so naïve to think that America would not have pockets of poverty right alongside its deep pockets of prosperity? Who could be so gullible to not suspect, even without the evidence of being there, that America has as many ghettoes as it has glittery mansions?

In a way, I must have always known it, but this trip was a way to give knowledge an experience. We were bearing witness to other American stories. And the plural is important here. After all, there is no single American accent, no single American city, no single American town, and perhaps no single American dream. Certainly there is no single American story. Everywhere in the world is ironically the same in this — in its lack of sameness. In any given place, several concurrent realities are always happening simultaneously. As we travelled, we spoke quite a bit about the idea of "American Exceptionalism." It seemed to me a ridiculous idea when confronted with the ever multiplying multiplicity of the American experience. Why was there this impulse to homogenize such a plethora of realities and then hold up the agreed upon version as unique? But once again, I thought, America isn't unique in this. Almost every culture has moments when it trumpets its own tired discourse of how exceptional it is. How many times have I heard the comment, "Only a Jamaican!" when one Jamaican has witnessed something that another Jamaican has done. How many national jokes are built on the formula "You know you're such-and-such when you do such-and-such." In Jamaica they would say, you know you're Jamaican when you point with your lips; or you know you're Jamaican when you ask for a glass of "ice water." That sort of thing. But I've heard similar jokes in Scotland and South Africa and Australia. All these countries have their own precious ideas of what is uniquely Jamaican or uniquely Scottish or uniquely South African or uniquely Australian.

When I pointed this out, that it was unexceptional for a culture to think of itself as exceptional, someone informed me that this would be a surprising idea to some Americans. I thought then — well, maybe they are exceptional after all!

The American realities we saw were various, but they had all been touched by a disaster of some sort. "Disaster" is not the most euphemistic word for death but it is a euphemism all the same. All the places we went to were dealing with the fact that people and things around them had either died or were dying and the response to this was various. Sometimes it was to write books and pamphlets (as Greg Guirard had done for the Atchafalaya families; some of his pamphlets even looked like funeral programmes) or it was to write plays (as John Biguenet is doing for New Orleans with his amazing trilogy; the second half of his play on the roof of a house, waiting for help, will stay with me for a long time) or it was to build monuments as they have done in Gettysburg Park — it seemed to me that here was a set of architects and builders who were trying to create grief spaces for themselves and their people.

By a "grief space" I mean to draw attention to something more than just a "grief state." I'm not so much interested in the feeling of grief (though this is important as well) as I am in the deliberate construction of a space to contain and in which to perform that grief. I am interested in the architecture, in the nails, and in the boards. The difference is this: to simply cry would be to enter a state of grief, but to cry at a funeral would be to enter a space of grief. Of course the two things are related. One must be comfortable with the state of grief to make a careful space for it, and then to enter such a space.

The poems I have been writing these past many years have in fact been grief spaces. The last collection was largely about my mother's passing. But I did not always think of the poems as spaces for sorrow, because again they were at times funny, and almost always they were hopeful. I know what my poems are now though, and there is perhaps a slight incongruity that I have been writing such poems in Britain. You see, it is not an unjustified stereotype to talk about English stoicism. There is this idea that to express grief too loudly is to be unseemly. Indeed, in the Anglican church in which my mother's funeral was held (the Queen of England is still the head of the Anglican church), the reverend would not allow the coffin to be open. An open coffin, he suggested, would excite people rather too much, and we wouldn't want to have that, would we? I am used to this privileging of sobriety and sublimation. In the aftermath of the train bombs of 2005, several Brits declared on TV that they were proud to just "get on with it," without much of a hullabaloo, not like the self-serving ruckus those ghastly Americans carried on with after 9/11!

It is also true that the standard British reaction to tragic news (whether that your mother died, or that you only have six months to live) is "Oh dear! Would you like a cup of tea?" But teacups are just as ridiculous containers for sadness as they are for storms.

What stereotypical English culture and my mother's reverend are afraid of is the state of grief, which can become an unmanageable thing. They would rather suppression than some unstoppable excess, which threatens to pull everything into its vortex. But what I am talking about here is grief that has in fact been organized. It isn't callous to point out that we can do this; if a grief space is built well, it allows us to explore and perform our sadness in healthy, thoughtful, poignant, uplifting, and sometimes even joyful ways.

America seems to get this in a way that I didn't. They have been building grief spaces, knowing that it is an important thing to do. How strange for me to finally come to this realization after I had constructed so many grief spaces myself: the thing I read at my mother's funeral, and an entire book of poems. I have read these poems on several occasions and at several festivals over the past year and ushered complete strangers into the grief space I had created but had never gone into myself.

On the penultimate day of our trip across America we had a public debriefing at the American University in Washington DC. Eduardo Halfón sat on the stage, his tonsure reflecting the big lights that were above him. Eduardo, not by virtue of age, but by virtue of a kind of nervousness that needed always to know that we were where we should be and that everyone was ok, had become the virtual father of the group. We had teased him by occasionally asking him stupid little things that a child might. "Eduardo, can we please use the bathroom? Eduardo, can we please have a candy?"or better still, "Eduardo, are we there yet!?"

On stage, Eduardo was trying to summarise our experience from Baltimore to Alabama. He did a good job though, in the end he appeared suddenly lost as if in a trance. The refrain he kept coming back to, the question he posed that he couldn't answer himself, was "Why us? Why writers?"

Again and again he asked it. Why us? Why writers? Soon he was pulling us all into this trance. We sat there, four of us in the audience, three others up there on stage with him, and each of us contemplating this question he had posed on our behalf. I do not know what was going through Vicente's or Alice's or Billy's or Adisa's or Madeleine's or Khet's mind. I know what I was thinking. I was thinking it was probably more important that we couldn't yet answer this question. I was thinking about my notebook filled with notes, and my camera's memory card filled with pictures, and all the thoughts that had been circling and circling round my head. And it seemed suddenly to me that I was being so goddamned contemplative and trying to be so goddamned smart, and not allowing myself to just be overwhelmed.

The two weeks had been that. Overwhelming. It had been an incredible and a perplexing sojourn, an uplifting and a heart-breaking journey. But in the end none of it made sense as a whole. I couldn't find a single narrative that had been running through everything — from the empty and crumbling Victorian houses of Baltimore, to the empty lots of New Orleans, to the story of the flustered birds that had dropped sunflower seeds all over the city after the hurricane, to the house that we had stood across from in Birmingham that had once belonged to Herschell Hamilton, "the bite doctor," a physician who had treated those who had been bitten by dogs during the Civil Rights demonstrations of 1963. Here at the end I was confronted with a kaleidoscope of images and realized that they didn't all go together. I thought of my small notes that were supposed to remind me of bigger stories; I thought of the hundreds of pictures I had taken, but there was no narrative — no story. There was just the overwhelm.

Two months have gone by since that trip, and in those two months I have travelled to other places. More places than I have ever been to in my life. I've gone to Africa and Australia and Asia. (It occurs to me that I have been to lots of places that start with the letter A.) The whole time, however, I have been thinking about those two weeks in Third World America and thinking about Eduardo's final unanswerable question: Why us? Why writers?

Eduardo, if I may: I think it is because we are elegists. Or at least, we often are. And this is just another way of saying we are in the business of creating grief spaces. Unfortunately, there are not many people who do this kind of work.

Eduardo, I am suddenly remembering Charlie Duff who also does important work. We met him in Baltimore, a silver-haired man who kept on telling us to "Look! Ask yourself, what is happening here?" Charlie Duff had trained to be a city planner but has become a developer instead, and the most rare kind — a developer with a soul. It would probably be more accurate to say that Charlie has become a reviver. He brings dead parts of his city back into life. But even Charlie would point out streets that would never come back to life. That is what he said, and we would hear again these exact words a few days later in

New Orleans. An old woman on a bus would point to abandoned hospitals and abandoned malls and abandoned neighbourhoods and she would tell us with a sad finality — that is never coming back.

Eduardo, I think that whenever a place vanishes, someone ought to create a grief space — not for the place, but for those of us who have lost the place. You see, before this trip I never fully appreciated that places could die like people. I thought that if a place died, it would do so slowly. Gradually. I never knew that a place could die right in front of our eyes even as we held on to its hand as if we were sitting by the bedside of our ailing mothers.

Eduardo, New Orleans is dead. It was washed away by an escaped lake. A new city is now growing where the old one had been, and the new city will keep the name. At least this time around, the name will be true, as John Biguenet assures us that this brand new New Orleans is not the one he grew up in.

Eduardo, the bayous are dead. Over one hundred of these magnificent swamps are buried permanently under the roads and the highways that the government thought were more important. And even if I were to take up a pickaxe right now and destroy those many miles of asphalt, the bayous and their birds and their alligators would not come back.

Eduardo, there are whole streets in Baltimore that are dead. The houses on these streets are empty and not even squatters will move in. The boards on their windows will not come down until the houses themselves fall. These streets will sink into the earth like Ancient Egypt, waiting for an archaeologist to rediscover it a thousand years from now.

Eduardo, the coast of Louisiana is dying. It is drowning every day as if it was a wary swimmer that could not manage another stroke. The landscape changes; it diminishes so quickly that cartographers cannot keep up. The lost bits of coast are never coming back. They have become a past tense. And what can we do about any of this but write elegies? What can we do but create grief spaces, in our own small ways? That is why us, Eduardo. That is why writers.

I have said already how this trip began — in an airport at night, sitting with Hugh after everyone else had arrived. It ended in almost the same way, in an airport at night, with Hugh, after everyone else had left. On that evening the tornados had just touched down in Alabama and the television sets mounted throughout the airport were reporting on it. Planes were being rerouted and passengers were nervous that they weren't going to make their flights.

But instead of airports and arrivals and airports and departures, I could signpost this journey in a whole other way. I could tell you that it began with a cemetery and then it ended with one.

On my first night, when the driver collected us, we drove an hour to Gettysburg. It was dark when we arrived, going on to midnight, and all the writers were already sleeping. Hugh directed me to my room and I went to bed. Although I was the last in, it seems I was the first up the next morning. I went outside and, now that things were not covered in darkness, I could see that we were on the edge of a cemetery.

I put on my running shoes and decided to go jogging through the Necropolitan landscape. Everything was beautiful and orderly. Billy Kahora would make mention of this in just a few hours, after I had finally met the group and we were getting ready for our first tour. Billy pointed to the sidewalks and noted how precisely the grass had been cut and how there was no hint of litter anywhere. I imagine that when Abraham Lincoln read his Gettysburg Address, one of the most beautiful elegies written, that the very grounds must have seemed holy. I would like to imagine that a few people were moved to tears, and that maybe an older woman came up to him after, held his hand and said, "It was a beautiful thing that you did today. It was an important thing."

I was, incidentally, more moved by the Gettysburg Address than I was by the physical park. I wonder if what it is, is that words hold grief better than landscapes — that words make better grief spaces than empty acres of land. I am thinking also of the letters of the Civil War soldiers that we read, letters whose syntax had become wobbly and eloquently incoherent as if they had been affected by the dying happening all about them.

If our journey began at Gettysburg, it ended at the Arlington National Cemetery, and I think it was appropriate that two cemeteries should stand on either end of our sojourn, like the embrace of parentheses, which is perhaps all this essay is — a parenthetical remark from someone on the outskirts of America looking in over the tombstones, inserting his small observations into a much bigger story.

My fellow writers may tell you how the issue of race seemed to come up at every stop and how it coloured everything, so to speak. This is true, but for me it was the dead who seemed to follow us everywhere. From cemetery to cemetery. It was the dead who kept on trying to speak. It was the dead who wanted a space in which we could remember them. From the fallen soldiers of Gettysburg, to the drowned people of New Orleans to our own recently departed family members, the dead followed us every step. It wasn't only my mother who haunted this trip across America.

There was Adisa's mother as well. By Adisa's account she had died bravely, pretending that she didn't know she was dying, pretending that she believed the doctor who told her everything would be okay. Her family in turn also pretended they didn't know she was dying, that they hadn't heard something quite different from the doctor who had told them flatly — everything was NOT going to be okay and that they should prepare themselves. But mother and family played their game, right up till the end, protecting each other from the pain of their mutual knowing.

And there was also Nataša's mother. By Nataša's account this Eastern European woman died as she had lived — pragmatically. She accepted the fact of her death and diligently planned the how and where of her memorial. On the day, everything went according to plan, except for the urn that was still inelegantly wrapped in its bubble-wrap. And when Nataša tells me the story of how the urn was brought out in front of everyone, its beauty hid behind plastic, and how no one had the presence of mind to rescue it from this indignity, she laughs and laughs, such a wonderful laughter, both light and dark, as if it could break at any second and tumble downwards.

This was supposed to be a travel essay, and I guess in a way it is. I went to America to see Baltimore and New Orleans and Louisiana, but where I finally arrived was at a place of my own creation — a grief space I had made almost two years ago. To enter it, I had to lock myself in a room, turn on my computer and then search for a file I knew was there. I was looking for that very funny thing I had written for my mother's funeral.

I opened the file and I read it aloud to myself. At the point when my voice broke, I did not stop it from breaking. I allowed it to tumble all the way down. I allowed myself into the grief space I had built and that my aunt had entered. My dear Vicente, you will be relieved to know I finally allowed myself to cry.

ALICE PUNG

Executing History

T. S. Eliot wrote, "I will show you fear in a handful of dust." If you were to pick up a handful of dust, knowing that there was a high possibility that you were holding on to the literal remains of half your family, the half you will never meet — all the cousins and aunts and uncles and grandfather that would have peopled your world but for the blunt force trauma of the Pol Pot regime — what does that mean? And if your father, standing there right next to you, tells you that this is where he carried and buried them a few years before your birth, when the floods came, when they starved to death, when they closed their eyes with nothing but the scraps of black-dyed pyjamas covering their backs minus the buttons, would you bend to touch this earth? And how do you react when your father tells you quietly and matter-of-factly, "The next year we planted crops in the same field. The rice grew twice as much, and twice as high." What does it mean to write about fall and recovery? How do we look at history and make it matter when the past is dead, and to start all over again sometimes means to leave it buried? These were the questions that preoccupied my mind for the past year, stemming from the trip I took with my father to Cambodia for the first time. A year later, I was standing in a different burial ground, still thinking about the same questions, but at the site of a different civil war that happened a 150 years ago. Gettysburg is a town gently yet persistently preserved in its history. The pre-Civil -War university, Gettysburg College (formerly known as Pennsylvania College), still stands today. The same building that was used as a war hospital on campus looks almost as it did a 150 years ago on the outside. The battlefields are all still there, left flat and verdant as they were during the battle. The copse of trees from which the Confederates aimed at the Union base is still planted in the exact same position. The wooden fences have been recreated to look as they did one and a half centuries ago. Everything is still, because it's not tourist season yet; and everything is quiet.

This had been one of the bloodiest battle sites of the Civil War, a war in which more American soldiers were killed in the course of battle than in the Vietnam and Iraq wars combined. A loss on the same scale today, according to the sources at the Civil War Museum, would equal six million casualties.

Gettysburg had been a rural farming town of twenty-two hundred and only one civilian was reported to have been killed during the battle — a woman named Jennie Wade who was baking bread in her house when she was hit by a stray bullet that went through two doors. The house in which she died is now a museum. It is incredible in this day and age to think that in a battle of fifty-one thousand military casualties, only one civilian was killed.

But this war was not a civil one, fought brother between brothers, as had been romanticised in the past for the purposes of achieving social cohesion in the new Union. This was clear when I saw photographs of piles and piles of amputated limbs, or pictures of all the bodies buried in shallow graves. As Professor Peter Carmichael of Gettysburg College led us through the battlefields, we stood in spots where thousands of men were killed in twenty minutes of battle, which later became the same place that the KKK held its rallies in the 1920s.

Today, confederate flags hang from shopfronts, and inside the souvenir stores you can buy grey (confederate) and blue (union) caps, Abraham Lincoln bobbleheads, and whole toy soldier packets for little children where they can re-enact the Civil War. I have to remind myself that this war was fought before the invention of plastic.

Yet almost every gift shop along Steinwehr Street advertises "Real Civil War Relics," which largely consist of buttons and bullets. Everything back then, in the mid-nineteenth century, seemed organic except for bullets and buttons, everything melted back into the ground. But bullets and buttons—these were the only relics that did not decompose. Here, you can buy a bullet for three dollars (or four dollars for an unexploded bullet). I held a bullet in my hand. Encrusted with the lime of age, it was white and heavy with a wide round tip. How strange to think that something so metallic, so inorganic, so tiny, could lodge in the living breathing mass of a person. These Civil War soldiers back then would not have looked up at the sky to imagine that a little over fifty years later, tonnes of metal would be able to float in the atmosphere, able to drop iron eggs that exploded on the ground. Human beings can bring inanimate objects to life, but they cannot bring living creatures back from death.

So we preserve all that we can—the names of the regiments, the nameless remains at Arlington National Cemetery, the Gettysburg battleground, the letters from dead soldiers. In 1862, a college-educated northern lieutenant named Rush P. Cady wrote about sacrificing lives upon the altar of one's country:

> The march of progress always goes through the battlefield. Good men have always fought to maintain & defend great principles. Good governments cost blood & treasure in the founding & also the preservation. The individual man is but a tool for the promotion of the progress & welfare of the whole race. [1]

---

1   Maurice Isserman, "From the Playing Field to the Battlefield," *New York Times,* 23 May 2011.

However, John Futch, a twenty-six-year-old illiterate Southern soldier who dictated his letters home, felt differently. He was a New Hanover County man who owned three slaves. In his letter dated 19 July 1863, to his wife, he had just witnessed his brother's death:

> Charley got kild and he suffered graideal from his wound he lived a night and a day after he was wounded we sead hard times thare ... I am all ... sick all the time and half crazy I never wanted to come home so bad in my life but it is so that I cant come at this time I want to come home so bad that I am home sick I want you to keep charleys pistol and if I ever git it back I will keep it ... I staid with Charley until he died he never spoke after he was woundid until he died I never was hurt so in my life[2]

John Futch's letters home reveal an increasing desperation, home-sickness, and escalating desire to be away from battle. His wife Martha's yearning for him sprawls across the pages ("dear husband I shal come to see you if you aint back by april for I want to see you veary bad"); but he wrote to tell her not to come to find him, reassuring her that he would be home soon. Shortly after the death of his brother Charley, Futch deserted the army. He was caught, sent back and executed in front of his fellow soldiers. The Confederate government made an example of John Futch's death:

> We do hope that the melancholy fate of these deluded men will ... put a stop to the crime of desertion from the army. ... Their names are disgraced forever, and around their memories will forever linger a dark stain that can never be blotted out.[3]

---

2   Letter from John Futch to Martha Futch and "Mother," July 19, 1863, accessed on the North Carolina Digital Collections, http://digital.ncdcr.gov/cdm4/document.php?CISOROOT=/p150 12coll8&CISOPTR=2581&CIS OSHOW=2579, North Carolina Department of Cultural Resources, accessed: 5 June 2011.

3   *The Raleigh Spirit of the Age,* reporting on "The Execution of Ten Men" (4 September 1863) in September 1963.

This was an era where post-traumatic stress didn't exist. Lieutenant Cady had left Hamilton College to fight in the war. While rallying his men on the first day of Gettysburg, he was struck by a minié ball and died of his injuries three weeks later. He was only twenty-two. Historians have asked whether his faith in heroic abstractions would also have survived if he too had survived the war. This was a time when personal feelings were subjugated for a greater cause, and the cause was meant to direct the course of a person's feelings. So what exactly was this greater cause? The survival of the Union, the fate of slavery, and the common rights of citizenship. Only two of these issues are resolved in the United States today.

Although there perhaps still exist some in the Southern states today who maintain that the Civil War was about the Southern states opposing the control of the new federal government, these states were largely agrarian economies dependent on slaves for the cotton trade. So this war was also undeniably about the right of Southern landowners to own slaves, which had been outlawed in the North in the very early part of the nineteenth century.

In the South, fewer than four slaves out of a hundred lived past the age of sixty. By the age of twelve, when a slave was sent to the fields, they had rotten teeth, worms, dysentery. Slaves, with their owners' consent, were allowed to marry; but their marriages were not recognised under law because they were considered chattels, not people. Preachers had to modify the wedding vows for them to till death or distance do us part,[4] because slaves had three to four masters in their lifetimes. In 1860, four million men, women, and children were slaves.

I went into Gettysburg Museum and saw the duplicate slave auction posters, which listed the slaves' ages, descriptions, and prices. Some who were of "unsound mind" or "infirm" cost around $200, others who

---

4   This is mentioned in a number of books about slave family relationships, such as Emily West's *Chains of Love: Slave Couples in Antebellum South Carolina* (University of Illinios Press, 2004) 64, and Catherine Adams and Elizabeth Hafkin Pleck, *Love of Freedom: Black Women in Colonial and Revolutionary New England* (Oxford University Press, 2010) 28.

were in their prime—and especially if they were of a "high yellow" colour—were valued at over a thousand dollars. Beneath the poster would be a line stating: Some cattle, and farm-stock also available at auction, and, As prices are so low, cash only.

Even after the Civil War and the abolition of slavery, human beings were still regarded as chattels. When we visited Birmingham, we were guided around the town by Pamela King, a professor at the University of Alabama who teaches a subject called "Mansions, Mines and Jim Crow." Founded in 1871, Birmingham was a post-Civil-War city, built during the middle of the Reconstruction era. Between 1875 and 1928, Alabama profited from a form of prison labor known as the convict-lease system. Under this system, companies and individuals paid fees to state and county governments in exchange for the labor of prisoners. Professor King explained that when the city passed its first vagrancy act, anyone not working the very moment he was spotted by police could be arrested and taken to the county jails, and then transported to the Birmingham mines. Between 20 to 43 percent of the miners died every year. Unlike slaves who had a value because they were personal property, these convicts were entirely expendable. More than 95 percent of county prisoners and 90 percent of state prisoners were African American, and whipping was the accepted norm for punishment.

From 1975 to 1979, Pol Pot of Cambodia and his Khmer Rouge soldiers also kept slaves, and they too did not buy or sell them. They all belonged to the revolution. The entire nation was divided up into different work collectives. Each collective consisted of a couple thousand people, and they were worked to death or executed in the fields. That is why that area and era is known now as the Killing Fields. My father, along with the entire population of Cambodia, was kept working in Democratic Kampuchea, as the country came to be known. "To keep you is no gain, to kill you is no loss" was the Khmer Rouge motto, drilled into the brains of every worker under the revolution, day in and day out. Pol Pot turned time back to Year Zero. He wanted to start civilisation from scratch, from a point of time that didn't exist anymore.

How do you write about a completely subjugated human being—who also happens to be your father and someone whom you love to no end—when you were not there, when you can only see the after-effects, which in your childhood and adolescence you took to be an excessive need to control? I had hoped that this trip would help me understand this part of our personal history a little better by allowing me to see the larger forces that shape or contort human nature.

What had kept my father alive? Perhaps human will is stronger than subjugation. This is what we would like to believe, as people of faith and reason. But it could also possibly be that even animals locked up and tortured try and stay alive. Thomas Jefferson wrote that main-taining slavery was like holding a wolf by its ears, too afraid to let go in case it bit the master. At what point does a human become an animal? When they are sold alongside animals? When they start eating food left out for pigs? When they scrabble against their ailing father for a piece of bread, as Elie Weisel wrote in *Night*? When they start eating scorpions and rats, as my father did? Or do they get to become human again when they survive? To survive means to stay alive, and sometimes staying alive means shutting off certain faculties. You reduce your existence to your five senses, because anything more would use up energy. Often, it is only after the traumatic event that your full spectrum of feeling sets in. When my father had to cut up his leather belt and boil it for hours, in secret, to feed to his family, it was as François Bizot wrote: "A man's life was reduced to his digestive tube."[5]

After the revolution, my family was lucky enough to arrive in a new country that accepted the shell-shocked, the frail, and the sick-at-heart: a heavily pregnant young woman (my mother), a seventy-two-year-old grand-mother and her son (my father) who buried bodies with the same hands that held a soft-bristled toothbrush to brush the baby

5   François Bizot, *The Gate*, translated from the French by Euan Cameron (The Harvill Press, London, 2003) 121.

teeth of his four children. All of us born in Australia, none of us slaves, subjugated citizens, or denied our human rights in any way.

From the "collectives" of the Killing Fields to raising four children in Australia, adjusting to a new social and political order could not have been easy for my parents. "We never thought much about the future when we were in Cambodia," my mother told me. "We just lived from day to day, in the same way, all our lives, until the war broke out." Now they get the newspaper, and dad reads through the lifestyle magazine section, mesmerised by the way people can choose to "style" their lives like their houses. My siblings and I were taught at school from a very young age, by well-intentioned teachers, that that we should dream large because we had infinite potential. Perhaps this was quite similar to the way American children are taught in schools, except for one significant difference: our individual aspirational narratives were never tied to the fate of our nation. Australia referred to itself as "The Lucky Country" when I was growing up, a recognition that life was a bit of a gamble and we just happened to be on top of things for once. But there was also a deep-seated acknowledgement that this could very easily shift. After all, we do not have "inspirational" presidents like Lincoln, Roosevelt, or Obama. There is a tendency to cut our tall poppies down. Before the rise of sporting idols, our national hero was Ned Kelly, a bushranger who wore a tin can over his head as armour until he was caught by the police and hung in the old Melbourne Gaol. Until his luck ran out.

I had not heard of the term "American exceptionalism" until I was in the States. Somehow, to cultivate the idea that a group of people can be the chosen ones, can be gifted with a mission, can be blessed with an abundance that other countries in the world do not have, is to deliberately cultivate in the national psyche a guppie memory. But this selective spring clean-out of the country's history has been so sucessful that it is difficult to imagine overseas that America — a country that presents itself to the rest of the world as a unified force imbued with immeasurable wealth, modernity, and power — was once a group of war-ring states divided by an ideology deep enough to rival that of North and South Vietnam in the 1960s. Of course, during the Vietnam War, the Civil Rights Movement was also taking shape in America. The Republican Party used to be "the Party of Lincoln" while the Democrats in the South had imposed racial segregation by law. Steadily and stealthily, the course of history crept on and allegiances that men had once believed were immutable, allegiances for which they had even died, were now reversing, cooling, shifting. So to believe in any form of exceptionalism is to follow a narrative along a straight trajectory, like a bullet.

Yet to live in America is to know that there are places that have it much worse. Perhaps that is why some poor people in Morgan City, Louisiana, and Alabama still have American flags planted firmly in the front yards of their properties, which house trailers or kit homes. Growing up in Melbourne, Victoria, we lived in similar suburbs, but no one ever planted an Australian flag in the front yard.

When they first arrived in Australia and before their blind pursuit of the Australian Dream, our parents had friends. Most of them survived the Killing Fields; some fought in the Vietnam War; some were conscripted, like one of my uncles who was pulled out of his village, an AK47 shoved in his hands. Life in a democracy was baffling. The women sighed a lot; the men were reticent. They were all scared of authority — the government, police, ticket inspectors on public transport, even parking inspectors. Sometimes they talked about the Black Bandits, which was what they called the Khmer Rouge. Yet with the glassy-eyed unfaltering optimism of a Gatsby, my father believed in the Great Australian Dream, which was very similar to the Great American Dream and all those "Great Dreams" of Democratic Western Countries, lands of the free and homes of the brave: the unfaltering faith that if you worked hard enough and never gave up, success was inevitable. This belief was their buffer against trauma and being stuck in the quagmire of the past.

Barbara Ehrenreich writes in "The Dark Roots of American Optimism" about how the Calvinism brought to New England by the white settlers seemed to be a "system of socially imposed depression," and how the movement towards positive thinking was a rebellion against the emotional austerity imposed by the Church and society. If you replaced the religious purpose with political motivation, the below description sounds eerily like the ideology of a socialist dictatorship:

> The task for the Living was to constantly examine "the loathsome abominations that lie in his bosom," seeking to uproot the sinful thoughts that are a sure sign of damnation. Calvinism offered only one form of relief from this anxious work of self-examination, and that was another form of labor — clearing, planting, stitching, building up farms and businesses. Anything other than labor of either the industrious or spiritual sort — idleness or pleasure — was a contemptible sin.[6]

Ehrenreich argues that the contemporary glo-white-smile brand of American optimism derived not from conformity but from a need to rebel against the Puritanical past. Instead of toiling to uproot evil from one's soul, one could work to enjoy the fruits of God's blessings. This was epitomised by the cheery and stoic wagon-progress mentality of the March sisters in *Little Women*, and as the decades progressed, it gave rise to writers like Emerson and later Norman Vincent Peale with his bestselling *The Power of Positive Thinking*. Yet when the complexities and problems with American identity and citizenship culminated in civil unrest, particularly in the sixties and seventies, people's peripheral vision could no longer be deliberately willed away. However, it could be distracted, with the ever-increasing lures of modern consumer society: things to own, things to be, things to eat.

6   Barbara Ehrenreich, "The Dark Roots of American Optimism," in *Bright-Sided: How Positive Thinking Is Undermining America* (Metropolitan Books, New York, 2009) 75.

The food in America looks and tastes good, in the way a child's drawing of food might be good: Yellow corn. Orange cheese. Red ketchup. Bright violet yoghurt. No green except diluted in lettuce leaves. What is the rationale for inventing food that contains less nutritional value than eating a leather belt? Perhaps the logic is that poor people are only going to get hungry again anyway, so let's just focus on the taste of the food. Give the indigent a little bit of happiness before they lose their teeth and die of heart attacks inside their kit homes.

Travelling through Louisiana, we stayed in the Bayou Breaux Bridge Bed and Breakfast. I spent two nights in the 1950s Elvis cabin, a cheery little space decked out entirely in the vintage optimism of the era — plastic flowers; crocheted bedspread; black and white Laminex tiles; and, of course, the King all over the mirrors, hanging from the wall with one finger pointed towards the firmament, and even as an enormous plaster bust on top of a cupboard. But we ate well. We went to the Crazy 'Bout Crawfish Cajun Café and feasted on boiled crabs, deep-fried Oreos, and deep-fried bread and butter pudding.

We went to New Orleans, the Big Easy, where the food was slow and the music was fast. We watched the filming of the TV series *Treme*, met the creator David Simon, drank hurricanes, and ate gumbo. Suddenly, this trip was beginning to become fun for me. It was beginning to remind me of my first trip to the States two years ago. Surrounded by its green paddocks and rows of cornfields, the University of Iowa was the ideal place for me to begin writing my first young adult book. Two years later, I completed a book about a man who survived a genocide in Cambodia and his relationship with his daughter. The story that emerged had not been the story I had set out to write at all. After handing in the final edits, I set off for my second trip to the United States, on this Fall and Recovery tour, feeling much trepidation and anxiety about whether I should have written what I had.

Then I met Madeleine Thien, our extraordinary Canadian writer whose recent book, *Dogs on the Perimeter*, deals with memory and grief and reads like a gentle, heart-starting poem. Maddie and I spoke a lot about Cambodia. She had visited the Killing Fields and the genocide museum a number of times, and I learned a lot from her about quiet courage. I also met Khet Mar, our Burmese writer who is on political asylum in Pittsburgh, and whose unfaltering knife-sharp sense of justice made me see the places we visited through new eyes. All my fellow writers taught me to see resilience in different ways.

We visited Greg Guirard, a Cajun fisherman, poet, writer, and photographer who has lived his whole life in the Atchafalaya Basin. "For a standard American," Greg told us, "if you're not making money, you're wasting time. For a real Cajun, "if you're not having fun you're wasting your life." His homeland in the Atchafalaya Basin had been logged to death, all the ancient cypress trees rooted out of existence a generation before his birth.

The Atchafalaya Basin is a part of the country that is very different from the rest of the United States. The Cajun people seem to be from a different era and place, when time moved slower and stoicism was a virtue. In 1604, their ancestors left France for Acadia, now known as Eastern Canada. After the British conquest of Acadia, they were deported in 1755, and first arrived in Louisiana a year later. Roy Blanchard, Greg's friend, told us that "a Cajun is a guy that's going to make it no matter what." Greg writes that "We Cajuns are being Americanized, and some of us don't like it at all. The Cajun Dream and the American Dream are not the same."

Greg and Roy took us out on a boat to the swamps of the Bayou. Greg's boat hauled up a catfish from a net. The catfish was enormous. At the bottom of the boat its gills opened and closed like someone flicking through the pages of a water-logged book.

Roy invited us to his house and showed us a turtle that he had caught, a beautiful slow creature that he was going to eat. These men had lived their whole lives out here, and their happiness seemed to derive from a hard-won acceptance of the vicissitudes of life as subsistence fishermen and hunters, yet a way of life that is in danger of being eroded, like the land of the Atchafalaya Basin.[7]

Most people have this deep-seated idea that a home is a place of warm comfort and simple safety, and so the idea of losing a home seems like losing all we have built in life, but it is more than that. Your home is a place where your suffering can take shelter. Homeless people in the street disturb us so because their misery is naked. There is nothing between them and the world, and the layers of grime and dirt and mental disquiet is often a result of being exposed alone in your suffering, whimpering in a place crowded with hurrying inhumanity. We hurry by because we are afraid, afraid there is nothing between us and them but very flimsy walls, nothing at all between the slave and the master but a layer of correctly colored epidermis, nothing between the right side of the war and the wrong side except whose trigger finger works faster under pressure, nothing between the living and the death but for the next breath.

Unless of course, you have faith. Perhaps the Church is a place where one's suffering can truly find sanctuary. So we visited two churches in the South. The first was an Evangelical church, with no altar and no cross. Instead, this sleek new place of worship consisted of just a modern hall equipped with all sorts of audio-visual equipment, and a rock band on stage. It was more a cross between a concert and a Tony Robbins seminar than a religious sacrament, and the pastor drilled into his predominantly white audience the lesson that they were God's Chosen People. They were there to make a difference — raising money for hurricane victims and evangelising. "You are the aroma of Christ, so spread that aroma far and wide!" bellowed the pastor. Then they sang a hymn: "God is Good, All the Time."

The women of the church told us how they selected New Orleans flood victims to shelter: only families were chosen, and these families

---

7   Greg Guirard, *Psychotherapy for Cajuns* (n/p, 2006) 11.

had to undergo background and criminal checks from the Sheriff's Department. They were given nine months to pull themselves together. These were people who had never before left their homes in New Orleans or set foot on a plane. Nine months to find jobs and restart their lives, or go back home. "It is sad," one lady of the church remarked to us. "Some of them couldn't do it. They just fell apart."

Of course, this is also what happens to "Chosen People" when disaster strikes—it is an enormous and sometimes unbearable blow to one's self belief. John Biguenet told us about the New Orleans doctors who took scalpels home while their surgeries were filling with floodwater; and how by the end of the weekend, they were dead. "Imagine this," John told us. "You're fifty-five years old. Your life has followed a certain successful and predictable path so far. You felt powerful and smart. But you have a mortgage on over a million dollars worth of surgical equipment in your clinic which you now can't repay because there are no more patients in New Orleans. You have a mortgage on a middle-class house. You have lost everything." Imagine being bogged down by your attachments. I have heard stories of wealthy families who piled themselves and their children into their Mercedes Benz when the city of Phnom Penh was being emptied of people. They drove their cars into creeks and rivers, choosing to die rather than confront the possibility of subjugation and hardship. Yet the Buddha said simply and unequivocally, *life is suffering*.

But take a look at us. We think we can control everything—our natural environment, other people, even our own bodies—and then when things seem beyond our control, when hurricanes hit, when levees break, when people die of dehydration on their rooftops, when we see masses of starving, huddled people, we recoil with horror. We don't think this sort of thing should happen. We insulate ourselves against the elements. Brad Pitt comes and builds a couple of beautiful, state-of-the-art, architecturally designed houses in New Orleans (even one shaped like a boat that will float away when the next flood comes), and that is the climax of the three-hour tourist "Hurricane Katrina Bus Tour." Ta-da! Recovery! We look through the bus windows, protected by a veneer of glass and moving vehicle, knowing that we are tourists who will go back to comfortable hotels, knowing we are writers who will go home to think about this long and deep and muster up the appropriate feelings of sympathy, moral outrage, and guilt.

"After all that's happened to them, they smile so much." People offer such polite charges of bravery to the people of Birmingham, Alabama, the people of New Orleans, the people of Burma, the people of Cambodia. We visit developing counties and remark about how happy the locals all look and how greedy we are back home, we toss the local children a few hundred riels and vow to change our own lives. Then we return to our quiet cul-de-sacs and forget. Maybe it is easier to take action to assuage our immediate feelings of guilt and feel good than it is to remember and reflect.

The second church we visited was the Sixteenth Street Baptist Church. This was the first all-black Baptist church of Birmingham, where many meetings during the Civil Rights Movement were held. Martin Luther King, Jr. visited this Church, and so did the Ku Klux Klan. On 15 September 1963, they planted explosives in the basement that killed four black girls — Addie Mae Collins, Cynthia Wesley, Carole Robertson, and Denise McNair — and injured more than twenty others. Twenty-six children at that time were walking into the basement assembly room to prepare for the sermon entitled "The Love That Forgives" when that bomb exploded, and what was left of the face of Christ on the stained glass window was a shattered hole.

Susan Sontag writes in *Regarding the Pain of Others*:

Someone who is permanently surprised that depravity exists, who continues to feel disillusioned (even incredulous) when confronted with evidence of what humans are capable of inflicting in the way of gruesome, hands-on cruelties upon other humans,

has not reached moral or psychological adulthood. No one after
a certain age has the right to this degree of innocence, of superfi-
ciality, to this degree of ignorance or amnesia. [8]

Jesus said blessed are the meek for they shall inherit the earth, while
poor Job sits there scraping his terrible skin with broken pieces of pot-
tery. Perhaps both can coexist without the need to find evil in Job or
excoriate the meek. Without immediately rushing to make sense of
suffering. This brings to the forefront a more fundamental question: is
there a need to make sense of suffering at all?

What if all my genocide-surviving father wants to do with his new
life is to start an electronics store in Melbourne, because in Democratic
Kampuchea all forms of technology had been wiped out except the
landmine, the AK47, and the electric fence around Tuol Sleng? What if all
my dad desires is to invest in a string of properties and confine himself
to a leafy suburb, happily believing that the worst thing that could
happen to me as a writer is a paper cut? What obligation then do I have,
as a writer, when I go back to dig up the past?

Last year when I visited Cambodia with my father, he was also
going to go with me to Tuol Sleng, the death and torture prison that
used to be an old primary school. In Tuol Sleng, faces stare at you from
the walls, photographs of prisoners before execution. Not just men, but
women with babies, children. Some of the faces have bloody noses,
others have eyeballs beaten out of sockets, all are still alive but know
they are going to die.

We never went in, never even came close to seeing the prison. Half-
way there and entirely unrelated to our visit, I vomited in my uncle's
car. I was just dehydrated, unaccustomed to the climate. The chauffeur
drove us straight back to the air-conditioned comfort of my uncle's
house, where my auntie sighed and said, "See, you shouldn't visit such
evil places. The bad spirits have gotten to you." They took me instead
to the Royal Palace with its floor of silver tiles, to Angkor Wat with

8   Susan Sontag, *Regarding the Pain of Others* (Picador, 2003) 89.

its apsaras flying all over the columns, and to their private beach at Sihanouk Hotel. My family wanted me to see recovery, not annihilation.

Yet how do I know about what is in Tuol Sleng prison? How can I describe the photographs, the bloodstains on the floor, the hairs stuck to the iron railings of the torture beds? These images are readily available to anyone — even a seven year old — if you entered in the right google terms. What makes the eyeballs of writers more legitimate? What makes historical suffering more "real" than historical "joy"?

And what does it mean to write about all this? Words are impermanent. Even books, which are physical objects, will get stuck in floods and become, as the playwright John Biguent said, "the heaviest objects imaginable." Professor Kent Gramm remarked to us during our meeting in Gettysburg, "There is the belief that history is nothing except language piling on top of language." What makes our transient thoughts real? If we stop thinking about trauma, does it exist? My cousins in Cambodia who survived Pol Pot can't remember a single thing about their childhoods during that era. Maybe the human body has a way of blocking off pain.

Blunt trauma needs to be alleviated by good health; love; success; and, dare I say, happiness. In America, in Louisiana, in Alabama, in Baltimore, in the Atchafalaya Basin, we did not see fulfilment of the American Dream. Sometimes we did not even see recovery. We met people like Greg Guirard who lamented the loss of their culture, Charlie Duff from Baltimore who mourned the disappearance of his stately city, and John Biguenet who reminded us that "the people of New Orleans have lived shoulder to shoulder with death since the founding of the city." We listened to people like Mr. Thomas Richard German, the seventy-six-year-old gentleman who led us through the Sixteenth Street Baptist Church where the four black girls were killed. Mr. German spoke about the changes he had seen in his lifetime and in his parents'. He told us how his father had worked for a white man and his children: "When that lil' boy or girl turned eight, my father had to call them by their title,

Master Alexander or Miss Emily." He told us about how during the fifties, sheriffs would pick up black men from the streets and castrate and kill them. How during the Civil Rights Movement, children were being arrested hundreds at a time and how the children actually enjoyed being taken in the police vans to the fairground to be processed. And how today, the most segregated day of the week in the United States is Sunday, when different groups go to their respective churches to hear about what makes a virtuous life, how to deal with loss, and how to make sense of uncertainty.

We must not forget that the United States of America was built through an era of uncertainty. Perhaps the man who came closest to understanding this uncertainty was Abraham Lincoln. It is unlikely that a man like that would ever be elected in today's current political environment. Lincoln lacked the charisma that is so necessary for television politics today, but more significantly he suffered from severe bouts of depression. "A tendency to melancholy," Lincoln wrote, "let it be observed, is a misfortune, not a fault." Yet that this mournful leader should deliver words that would rouse a nation at war defies all modern perceptions that depressed people are lackadaisical, are passive, and should be heavily medicated. It also makes me wonder whether American culture now puts too much emphasis on the emotions, as if they were the sole barometer of one's existence. In order to be a respected independent and adult human being, we are taught to be affirmative and preface our sentences with "I feel," "I think," "I know." What if there was just feeling, thought, and knowledge that did not belong to "me" or "I"? Then perhaps we would be more forgiving of self-doubt, sadness, reticence. They would not have to talk all the time to justify ourselves. And perhaps then, melancholia would not be a personal fault but a misfortune.

In his 1863 Gettysburg address, Lincoln said: "The brave men, living and dead, who struggled here, have consecrated it, far above our poor power to add or detract." This address, less than three hundred words long, endured throughout history as one of the most powerful speeches of all time. These words move because Lincoln does not try and "own" these men or their deaths. Lincoln does not cloak their cadavers in posthumous finery.

Standing on the battlefields of Gettysburg was an emotional experience for me. For a year, I couldn't write about the field in Cambodia and its dust of people without feeling like I was making them up, because I did not know them. All the buried cousins and all the starved uncles, all the small babies. All those meaningless deaths leaving behind nothing. I think perhaps this is what Lincoln means by our "poor power to add or detract." Lincoln understood what it was like to rise above emotion without superimposing optimism. Involuntarily blinkered by depression all his life, Abraham Lincoln never voluntarily willed away his peripheral vision.

I felt very lucky to have taken part in this tour. What amazed me most was that the U.S. Department of State would take a group of writers from around the world to show them not the best parts of the country—the thriving industries, the lively culture and art, and the booming cities—but the side of the country in the shadows. Perhaps no other country in the world would open itself up so liberally to literary ambassadors from other nations. Through the University of Iowa's Writers in Motion program, freedom of speech in America is real, and it thrives.

On my flight returning to Australia, my thoughts about my two-week journey were interrupted by my neighbour. I was seated next to a middle-aged gentleman who had teeth as white as a picket fence. He was everything an accomplished American man should be. Son of strict Eastern-European immigrants, he defied his parents' expectations and married a girl with hair the colour of cornfields. At one point in his life, he was sleeping in his car because his father had kicked him out of home. So he started his own business. Both his sons became professional sportsmen, which was why he was heading down to Australia, to see one of them perform in a world championship. He told me that anything was possible if you only worked hard enough for it, and believed in it enough, and were a decent person. He asked me what I had been doing in the States for two weeks, and I told him that I had been looking at disaster and resilience. A few hours before our plane landed, he asked me extensive questions on how he would go about writing his life story. But I had a creeping suspicion that he already knew how.

We had started our journey on a battleground in Gettysburg, and ended it in a burial ground at Arlington General Cemetery in Washington where the past was set in stone monuments, to be travelled across through well-paved pathways. Between these hushed places, we visited cities and heard the voices of people in these cities. We saw the parts of America where people were trying to eke out a life, trying their best to retain their separate cultures, people mourning loss, people being honest and resilient in quiet and unassuming ways. People forgotten by the narrative of quick success that is pivotal to the popular culture of the States today. The melancholy president, the common soldier, the Cajun fisherman, the middle-class church mother, the son of the Civil Rights Movement, and the optimistic father — all these people formed part of a common history. Before we left New Orleans, John Biguenet told us that "art is not about opinion. It is about human beings living."

FURTHER RECOMMENDED READING

Barbara Ehrenreich, *Smile or Die: How Positive Thinking Fooled America and the World* (Granta, 2009): Published in the USA as *Bright-Sided: How Positive Thinking Is Undermining America,* Ehrenreich began to write this book after she was diagnosed with breast cancer and realised that there were sections of society that truly believed that positive thinking would cure their illness. Note that the American version of the book does not use the word "Die" in the title, and the subtitle reads a bit like a disclaimer.

Susan Sontag, *Regarding the Pain of Others* (Picador, 2003): This book is about war, and the history of how images of war are used. Before the invention of the camera, war was documented by journalists. Before the invention of video, war was seen only in still images.

Kent Gramm, *November: Lincoln's Elegy at Gettysburg* (Indiana University Press, 2001): We met Professor Gramm in Gettysburg, and this fascinating book is a collection of essays about pivotal speeches and moments in U.S. history that happened in the month of November.

Greg Guirard, *The Land of the Dead Giants* (self-published, 2001, English and French edition): We met Greg in the Atchafalaya Basin and were mesmerised by his stories about Cajun culture in Louisiana. This novel has been turned into a play and is about a family trying to keep their traditions alive in a world of ever-escalating change.

E Benjamin Skinner, *A Crime so Monstrous: Face to Face with Modern-Day Slavery* (Free Press, 2008), which shows that slavery still exists today. Skinner actually goes around the world meeting slave dealers to buy slaves, to show how possible it is to buy the life of another human being.

Wallace Terry, *Bloods: Black Veterans of the Vietnam War — an Oral History* (Presidio, 1985): This is an incredible testimony of twenty African-American soldiers who fought in the Vietnam War, while back in their own country the Civil Rights Movement was still going on and Martin Luther King, Jr. had been assassinated.

John Biguenet, *Rising Water* (a play): We met Professor John Biguenet at Loyola University, New Orleans, after having read his Pulitzer Prizenominated play, *Rising Water,* which documents the effect of the breach of the levees after Hurricane Katrina on an old couple who have lived in New Orleans all their lives.

The Grand Tour:
In the Shadow of James Baldwin

"Thou knowest this man's fall; but thou knowest not his wrastling."
— John Donne, *Biathanatos*

1

"Just look," Charlie Duff said to us one night. "All I want is for you to look." It was late, and he was driving us — novelists Eduardo Halfón, Vicente Groyon and me — back to our hotel in Baltimore "I don't see anything," Ed said as we idled at an intersection, peering into the stillness. The light changed. We continued, down one street and then another, past parking lots without cars. I saw windows without any lights, and then windows without any windows. Charlie kept driving. All the row houses on every side were boarded up or condemned. On and on it went. It was as if some disaster had struck this place, and the residents had been hurriedly whisked away. Home after home, one after another, stood empty, empty. We circled a neighbourhood park, it was wild and overgrown. "Oh my God," I said.

Nothing moved. We kept going, circling the nearly 15,000 abandoned homes of West Baltimore.

We saw a boy standing in a doorway, hands in his pockets. The boy watched us as we watched him: as if he were a moon of Jupiter. As if we were a passing airplane. And then he, or we, disappeared.

Ed, Vicente, and I — from Guatemala, the Philippines, and Canada — belonged to a larger group, invited by the U.S. State Department and Iowa's International Writing Program (IWP) to take part in a study tour of the mid-Atlantic and American South.[1] Adisa Bašić, Khet Mar, Alice Pung, Billy Kahora, Kei Miller, and Sahar Sarshar—from Bosnia, Burma, Australia, Kenya, Jamaica, and Washington, DC, respectively—as well as two hosts, Nataša Ďurovičová and Hugh Ferrer, from the IWP, rounded out our circle.

Months earlier, our shared itinerary had been written. Travel money had been released from the Bureau of Educational and Cultural Affairs. Logistics and flight plans were missived to us in emails brief and long. We would begin our journey in the fields of Gettysburg, where 50,000 Americans lost their lives in three days of "nasty, untidy, brutal" battle and where Abraham Lincoln had issued a challenge to America: to remain unified and, in so doing, confront the nation's unfinished business, to make this "new birth of freedom"—a government of the people, by the people, for the people—a lasting reality. After Gettysburg, we would journey south to Baltimore, New Orleans, Morgan City, the Atchafalaya Basin, and Birmingham.

A website sprung up. We were instructed to blog. We were instructed to read. PDFs flourished on a dedicated url: essays on Robert F. Kennedy, Frederick Douglass, urban decay, and the disaster of Hurricane Katrina, as well as works by Barbara Ehrenreich, James Baldwin, and John McPhee.

From the emails and correspondence leading up to this tour, I had a sense that the powers that be (State Department "bigwigs," as one of our hosts called them) had something to unveil to us, a narrative that would challenge our preconceived ideas about the United States. They would show us what was broken, or had once been broken, they would show us the intricate webbing of America, a story told by individuals, cities, waterways, and communities.

---

1   Writers in Motion was organized by the International Writing Program at the University of Iowa. The Bureau of Educational and Cultural Affairs at the U.S. Department of State covered all accommodation and travel costs for the writers. No honorarium or salary was paid, but we each received a modest per diem to cover food and miscellaneous expenses. In return, we were asked to write an essay for which we would be paid $500.

I was surprised, and proud, to be a part of it all. Eight writers and one filmmaker, brought to America by Americans and tasked with a simple brief: "How do writers contextualize and sort through destruction, crisis, and recovery? How do they distill essential and accurate truth from disaster? Read the fall," we were told. "Write the recovery."

At that time, the spring of 2011, I had just published a novel about the aftermath of the Cambodian Civil War, and I had spent five years shuttling between Montreal and Phnom Penh, and also the city of Beirut, where my boyfriend had lived ten years of the Lebanese Civil War. Recovery abounded in both those countries, though it was never simple, and often it was not just. In America, I hoped to see how recovery and justice informed one another, how recovery was enacted in a nation where each citizen was assured fundamental rights, equality, before the law.

Arriving in Maryland, greeted by our hosts who had flown in from Iowa, I met the other writers for the first time. They were camped out beside the luggage carousels, around a table busy with paper cups and cellophane wrappers. All of us, except for Ed and Adisa, had spent a semester at the University of Iowa at some point in the last five years. We were poets and fiction writers and essayists, and our suitcases were full of books. I felt immediately happy, immediately at home. With Khet Mar, I went to assess the refrigerated sandwiches. Khet told me that, two years ago, she had left her native Burma and now, with her young family, she lived in Pittsburgh's City of Asylum. I told her how, in the aftermath of Cyclone Nargis, I had attempted to cross the border from northern Laos into Burma but had been refused a visa. We stared for a long time at the sandwiches and then opted, instead, for cookies, chocolate, and tea.

The next morning, the last of our group arrived. Alice Pung had flown in from Australia, and now she appeared at breakfast, glowing with warmth and energy.

Together, we set out for the fields of Gettysburg. We listened as historian Peter Carmichael, director of the Civil War Institute, remarked, in passing, on the mandate of the National Park Service. This year marks the 150th anniversary of the Battle of Gettysburg. These grounds, the NPS believes, are "a symbol of America's struggle to survive as a nation" and their responsibility, as caretakers, is to return the battlefield, "as closely as possible to its 1863 appearance."[2] In short, to preserve the grounds as they were 150 years ago.

Rolling hills, cannons, and soaring monuments surrounded us; even the trees — their very number, size, and location — were carefully manicured to provide an accurate backdrop for Civil War re-enactors.

We stood uncertainly on the grass. Of the future, and of Lincoln's challenge, "to make a new birth of freedom," neither the trees nor the hills could speak.

"What do you see?" Charlie Duff asked us. It was Day Four, Wednesday morning in Baltimore, and we were standing in a tranquil courtyard. April sunshine warmed our heads. Adisa and Kei sat on the swings, their toes against the concrete landing keeping them anchored and still.

In his forest green sweater, Charlie waited patiently. For the last 17 years, Charlie has worked to revitalize Baltimore's inner city. He does this by working as a non-profit developer, raising money, buying back historic buildings and restoring them.

I studied the landscape and saw a mini-Boston, a thriving, upscale, urban neighbourhood.

"Keep looking," he said.

I saw the confident beauty of a North American city.

Charlie smiled.

With a calmness that belied his subject, Charlie told us about an earlier city and a different world, a turn-of-the-century Baltimore in

---

2 "Preserve Gettysburg | Gettysburg Preservation: A Sacred Trust," www.gettysburgfoundation.org (accessed May 15, 2011).

post-Civil War America. Renowned for its monumental architecture, Baltimore had been both a shipping centre and a bullish industrial power, manufacturing everything from men's clothing to sheet iron to tin. Black families had arrived from the southern States, part of the Great Migration that brought 1.5 million African Americans into the north between 1910 and 1930.[3] In the years after the Second World War, another five million African Americans followed.

Forbidden from buying land, black workers and their families crowded where they could. "Here," Charlie said, nudging the grass with his foot, "a ghetto had taken root." "By 1930," the historian Elizabeth Wilkerson wrote, "some 165,000 coloured people were living in Harlem, packed so densely that some tenants had to sleep in shifts — as soon as one person woke and left, his bed was taken by another.'"[4]

The buildings here, Charlie told us, were just as beautiful as the best parts of Baltimore: stone and brick row houses and elegant garden apartments. But, as population density increased, these homes had to be subdivided, then subdivided again.

By the 1950s, young families were crowded into single rooms and tenements. Even when they were able to afford it, African Americans were prevented, through mortgage discrimination and redlining, from buying property.[5] The Federal Housing Authority's own manual recom-

---

3 "'They left as though they were fleeing some curse,' wrote the scholar Emmett J. Scott. 'They were willing to make almost any sacrifice to obtain a railroad ticket, and they left with the intention of staying.'... Over the course of six decades, some six million black southerners left the land of their forefathers and fanned out across the country for an uncertain existence in nearly every other corner of America." Wilkerson, Elizabeth, *The Wealth of Other Suns: The Epic Story of America's Great Migration* (New York: Random House, 2010).

4 Wilkerson, 249.

5 "Mortgage discrimination is the practice of banks, governments or other lending institutions denying loans to one or more groups of people primarily on the basis of race, ethnic origin, sex or religion. One of the most notable instances of widespread mortgage discrimination occurred in United States inner city neighbourhoods from the 1930s up until the late 1970s. There is evidence that the practice still continues in the United States today." Wikipedia contributors, "Mortgage discrimination," *Wikipedia, The Free Encyclopedia*, http://en.wikipedia.org/wiki/Mortgage_discrimination (accessed May 31, 2011). Recent studies have shown that this discrimination is still in force: "A study by the Center for Responsible Lending, a nonprofit research group based in North Caro-

mended neighbourhood restrictions that would prohibit "occupancy of properties except by the race for which they are intended... Schools should be appropriate to the needs of the new community, and they should not be attended in large numbers by inharmonious racial groups."[6]

"White Americans," Charlie told us, "have been willing to make almost any sacrifice so as not to live beside black Americans." In a subterfuge called "blockbusting," real estate agents arranged for a black family to move into a white neighbourhood. White homeowners panicked. Convinced that their streets had been infiltrated, they put their homes up for sale. Many lost as much as half the value of their properties. One economist found that "each black arrival led to 2.7 white departures."[7] Aided by spreading highways and government incentives to grow the suburbs, this "white flight" changed, perhaps forever, the nature of American cities.

In the courtyard, Charlie held our full attention. We were surrounded by greenery and blossoming trees; there were strings of birds on the overhead wires.

To protect the remaining white neighbourhoods, the city of Baltimore resorted to extreme measures. In 1962, they bulldozed this entire street. A small park was built where we now stood, the remaining blocks were left vacant. "A firebreak," Charlie told us, "used to keep the fire from spreading, to prevent the races from mixing." He gestured upward with his coffee cup. "And it worked."

Baltimore was not alone. In Dearborn, Michigan, the mayor told a receptive audience, "Negroes can't get in here. Every time we hear of a

lina, examined 50,000 subprime loans nationwide and found that blacks and Hispanics were 30 percent more likely than whites to be charged higher interest rates, even among borrowers with similar credit ratings. A report released in March by the Neighborhood Economic Development Advocacy Project and other groups found that in New York, blacks were five times and Hispanics almost four times more likely to pay higher interest rates for home loans than whites." "Studies find disparities in mortgages by race," *New York Times*, October 15, 2007.

6　*Ibid.*

7　Boustan, Leah Platt (2010). "Was Postwar Suburbanization 'White Flight?' Evidence from the Black Migration." *The Quarterly Journal of Economics*, 125 (1): 417-443.

Negro moving in, we respond quicker than you do to a fire."[8] Journalist Robert Caro notes that, prior to the building of New York's Gowanus Parkway, city planners argued, dishonestly, that the intended development site was blighted. They then proceeded to lay "a concrete slab on top of lively, bustling Third Avenue, [burying] the avenue in shadow, and when the parkway was completed, the avenue was cast forever into darkness and gloom, and its bustle and life were forever gone."[9] Down in Birmingham, interstate highways were built directly through black neighbourhoods, which "eventually reduced the populations to the poorest proportion of people financially unable to leave their destroyed community."[10]

"They trying to tear down our homes, brother," a young San Francisco man tells James Baldwin in the 1963 National Educational Television documentary *Take This Hammer.* "Wait, wait, wait, let me tell you. Now they talking about better jobs, jobs right here. You want me tell you what kind of jobs they gonna give us? They're gonna let us tear down on own homes. That's the job we're getting. And you know what they gonna pay us? Let me tell you want they're going to pay. They're going to pay you $2 an hour... They'll help you tear down your own home. It's a job, temporarily. And then what you going to do? Where you going to live? You're not going to live anywhere. They're not even in the process of trying to tell you where you're going to live. All they're talking about is tearing down your house."[11]

By 1970, economist David Cutler writes, "the average black in urban America lived in a neighbourhood that was 68 percent black."[12]

---

8   Wilkerson, 378.

9   Caro, Robert, *The Power Broker: Robert Moses and the Fall of New York* (New York: Knopf, 1974) 522.

10 Connerly, Charles E., "From Racial Zoning to Community Empowerment: The Interstate Highway System and the African American Community in Birmingham, Alabama," *Journal of Planning Education and Research,* 22.2 (2002): 99-114.

11 Moore, Richard, *Take This Hammer,* KQED and National Educational Television, 1963, Youtube.

12 Cutler, David M., Edward L. Glaeser, and Jacob L. Vigdor, "The Rise and Decline of the American Ghetto," *The Journal of Political Economy* 107:3 (1999) 455-506.

Forty years later, we drove past the boarded-up, windowless, degraded houses of West Baltimore, a neighbourhood chronicled in David Simon's enduring and devastating series, *The Wire*. Baltimore, Simon said, is home to the "the urban underclass," expendable people, citizens for whom the country has no use. *The Wire*, he said, was not a story about America, but ...about the America that got left behind... And certainly the ones who are undereducated, who have been ill-served by the inner-city school system, who have been unprepared for the technocracy of the modern economy, we pretend to need them. We pretend to educate the kids. We pretend that we're actually including them in the American ideal, but we're not. And they're not foolish. They get it. They understand that the only viable economic base in their neighbourhoods is this multibillion-dollar drug trade.[13]

Five years ago, Simon turned his attention to New Orleans, in particular, the historic neighbourhood of Faubourg Treme. In the 1960s, an interstate highway, I-10, was built straight through the middle of Treme's Claiborne Avenue, a wide promenade and the heart of the neighbourhood's business district. "They just took down hundreds and hundreds of homes where families used to live," said house builder Irving Trevigne. "They just got rid of 'em, displaced the people. Claiborne and mixed neighbourhoods like that. They'd create black projects and white projects. They made the city so it'd be like the rest of the country. They separated the people." Residents with money packed up and left for the suburbs, and old, historic neighbourhoods, like Faubourg Treme, fell into a shattering decline. Trevigne recalled, "In the 80s, crack cocaine just tore the families up. Drugs anywhere. I seen the whole thing change. We used to hear this gunfire every night. And I don't mean just plastic pistols. I'm talking about automatic weapons. Boom, boom, boom, boom, boom."[14]

---

13   Moyers, Bill, "The Straight Dope: Bill Moyers interviews David Simon," *Guernica*, April 2011.

14   Logsdon, Dawn and Lois Eric Elie, dirs., *Faubourg Treme: The Untold Story of Black New Orleans*, Serendipity Films, 2008.

"What we're not good at," Charlie concluded, looking out at our mixed group, hunched together, wordless, "is race." This, he said, was the great historical fact of America.

I stood in this leafy garden and tried to see beyond the trees and sunshine, into the things he spoke of, the history not visible to the naked eye: all the families and workers who once lived here, now dispersed to lives and destinies in other streets, other waters.

2

Three centuries ago, Richard Lassel, an English priest, articulated the spirit of the Grand Tour. He imagined a journey, undertaken with a knowledgeable guide or tutor, whose main purpose would be "to understand classical civilisation through a direct contact with its main centres."[15] In the years that followed, men and women of leisure, young entrepreneurs and budding statesmen, writers from Stendhal to Goethe to Henry James, went abroad to witness the social, political, and cultural realities of their time: "They came too, and perhaps above all, for [Italy's] ancient heart of darkness, for the ruins that speak of Rome."[16]

When Alexis de Tocqueville arrived on the shores of New York in 1831, he cast aside the binoculars of the Grand Tour and trained his sights on the revolutionary present. "It is not, then, merely to satisfy a legitimate curiosity that I have examined America; my wish has been to find instruction by which we may ourselves profit... I confess that in America I saw more than America; I sought the image of democracy itself, with its inclinations, its character, its prejudices, and its passions, in order to learn what we have to fear or to hope from its progress."

---

15 De Divitiis, Gigliola Pagano, "Art and Economics in the Grand Tour," originally published in Italian in *Rivista del Centro Internazionale di studi dell'Architettura Andrea Palladio*, 12, 2000, pp. 127-141. www.eh.net/XIIICongress/Papers/deDivitiis.pdf (accessed June 14, 2011).

16 Gualdoni, Flaminio. "Grand Tour," *Atlante dell'arte italiana*. www.atlantedellarteitaliana.it/index.php?essay=2&lang=english (accessed June 14, 2011).

Men had reason to believe, he said, that society was bending inexorably towards equality, and that this movement, "with ease and simplicity," was finding its most evolved form in the United States.[17]

Now, as our group moved from place to place, on a tour organized and imagined by American citizens, Charlie's words resonated in every city. "What's happening here? What's *really* happening? Try to see."

When we arrived back to our hotel in downtown Baltimore, a windy night had fallen. I stayed in my little room and tried to read, but the images of what we had seen troubled my mind, not because the issues of race and marginalization were so surprising but, rather, because they were so disconcertingly familiar. "In order to have a conversation with someone," the visionary American author James Baldwin wrote, "you have to reveal yourself."[18] So let me make this small digression, into the world that I come from, which has a history parallel to Baltimore's and to a number of American cities. My childhood was spent on the border of Vancouver's Downtown Eastside. Skid Row, my parents called it, just as everyone else did, not quite accepting that these were the streets we frequented. Skid Row, before it became Skid Row, was once the premier commercial district of Vancouver, gateway to the bustling seaport and national railway line. But, as in Baltimore, around these ports of industry, an impoverished and crowded community had come into existence. In the 1950s, the city tried to follow in the footsteps of its American counterparts. It declared Skid Row's adjoining neighbourhood, Strathcona, a slum, and earmarked it for demolition. Six hundred homes were scheduled to be bulldozed; in their place, a freeway overpass would be constructed. Residents from every part of Vancouver vociferously protested these plans and, in 1967, in nothing short of a small miracle, the protesters won. City Hall retreated and the demolitions never happened.[19]

---

17   de Tocqueville, Alexis, *Democracy in America,* trans. Henry Reeve (New York: Penguin, 2003) 22.

18   Baldwin, James, "Notes for a Hypothetical Novel," *James Baldwin: Collected Essays* (New York: The Library of America, 1998) 228.

19   "The History of Metropolitan Vancouver," www.vancouverhistory.ca (accessed May 30, 2011). http://www.vancouverhistory.ca/chronology1967.htm

I was eight years old when I started school in Strathcona, and it was the early 1980s. A man or woman, high, leaning against the other side of the schoolyard fence, prophesying, raging, or laughing, was not something to worry about. Needles in the grass were not oddities, they were barely worth mentioning. With a population that was nearly half immigrant and a quarter First Nations, with levels of poverty unheard of in the rest of Canada, with open drug use in the streets, this community may have struck the outsider as a ghetto but, if you lived within it, it did not seem this way.

When my father gave me 90 cents each day for the return bus fare to school, I took them all in nickels so that I could buy candy from the corner store and satisfy the cravings in my stomach. To do so, I had to cheat the bus driver. He never checked the fare box, never acknowledged his passengers, and was, I think now, in the grip of a terrible depression. At the time I was only too glad to escape his notice; the bus lurched forward, swaying with the mass of the young, the drunk, the agitated, and the deluded, and I would eat my candy slowly, pacing it out for the ride home.

Years passed. My parents separated; my mother worked three jobs, and my siblings moved away from home as soon as they could. I walked and walked, and then kept walking, I couldn't stop looking at the city I knew so well, wondering why this park was so deserted, or why all these immigrants ended up in this small corner of the city, or what kept me from crossing into Vancouver's wealthy west side, as surely as if there had been a wall? Why did I live in a coastal city and never go the beach? Why did I not feel that it was unjust that some people lived in estates surrounded by manicured shrubbery, while others lived on streets that, as my cousin said, "looked like Beirut or East L.A." I loved my neighbourhoods (unable to afford increasing rents, my mother moved us every other year), and would not have traded them for all the shrubbery in the world, but it turns out I did not know a fraction of what was going on around me.

A generation ago, James Baldwin wrote movingly about his struggle to understand America, his country. He held fast to the belief that the writer "must find the terms of our connection, without which we will perish...."[20] Every society," Baldwin wrote, "is really governed by hidden laws, by unspoken but profound assumptions on the part of the people, and ours is no exception. It is up to the American writer to find out what these laws and assumptions are... The time has come, God knows, for us to examine ourselves, but we can only do this if we are willing to free ourselves of the myth of America and try to find out what is really happening here."[21]

Throughout the 1980s and up until 2002, more than 60 women in the Downtown Eastside disappeared. For decades, their deaths were not investigated; many of these women were drug users or sex trade workers and, according to authorities, such people periodically disappear only to resurface in another city, or back on the streets. In 2007, a man was finally convicted of six murders; an attempt to try him for another 29 failed. A further 39 cases remain outstanding. Scholar and writer Elliott Leyton described the "bland, racist, sexist and classist prejudices buried in Canadian society: an institutionalized contempt for the poor, for sex trade workers, for drug addicts and alcoholics, for aboriginal people."[22] Here, too, were hidden laws I had to force myself to recognize.

When I was 19, I met a street nurse who had spent her entire adult life providing care to residents of the Downtown Eastside. She and her colleagues did HIV and STD testing in clinics, out of vans, and on foot. They provided counselling, distributed condoms, administered methadone treatment and antiretrovirals, and handed out clean needles. Since 2003, the Downtown Eastside has been home to Insite, North America's only safe, legal, drug injection site. In Canada, there is some

---

20   Baldwin, "Notes for a Hypothetical Novel," *Collected Essays,* 229.

21   Baldwin, "The Discovery of What It Means to Be an American," *Collected Essays,* 142.

22   Elliott Leyton, as quoted by Gabor Mate, "Images of Our Shadow Side," *A Room in the City: Photographs by Gabor Gasztonyi,* (Vancouver: Anvil Press, 2010).

resistance to Insite (its license to work above the law is permanently in danger), but by and large it is supported by the province, the city, and those, like myself, with a connection to the neighbourhood. The philosophy at work is based, not on the all-out aggression of a merciless drug war, but on a policy of harm reduction. Shalyn Shula, another nurse working in the neighbourhood, put it this way, "You cannot make things perfect in the Downtown Eastside. You can only accept what is here and try to make the residents' lives as happy and healthy as you can."[23]

For families like my own, the neighbourhood was a brief stop; immigrants moved on and moved out. When I started university, my mother settled in the distant suburbs where she lived until she passed away, too young, at the age of 58. Sometimes, now, when I return to the Downtown Eastside, I fear that it will never change, that this prison, this ghetto, exists in every country, in every age. Still, the community is strong here, and it endures.

This year, we have a prime minister who once said, "Providing for the poor is a provincial, and not a federal, responsibility."[24] Even now, some leaders believe they are fulfilling their duties when they leave a part of the population to drown.

"I was icily determined," Baldwin wrote, recalling his childhood self, "never to make my peace with the ghetto."[25]

3

On August 29, 2005, the levees of New Orleans were breached in more than 50 locations, a catastrophic disaster caused by design failures "so obvious and fundamental" that the United States Army Corps of Engineers would finally, after months of about-facing, admit some

---

23 Juschka, Amy, "Nursing the Neediest: A street nurse reflects on caring in the Downtown Eastside," *LPN Café.* http://www.lpncafe.ca/s_41.asp (accessed May 12, 2011).
24 "A selection of controversial Harper quotes compiled by Tories," *Globe & Mail,* April 26, 2011. Web.
25 Baldwin, James, "Down at the Cross," *Collected Essays,* 300.

culpability. Steel sheets that should have been 65 feet were instead, on average, 17 feet. To save money, some were as short as four, sunk into alluvial silt that had the consistency of coffee grounds.[26]

"People think we got hit by a hurricane. We got *missed* by a hurricane. The hurricane went east," one resident said.[27]

On Monday night, after the raging winds of Katrina had passed, the water began pouring in, over the levees and, stunningly, beneath them. The pressure was not great, the force of the hurricane in New Orleans was measured at Category 2, perhaps even Category 1, the lowest intensity.[28] Yet the levees bordering Lake Pontchartrain gave way and water began pouring into the city. It was the middle of the night. No warnings came over the radio. In some neighbourhoods, houses drowned in a matter of minutes. In others, the water rose slowly and, if residents were lucky enough to have woken, they moved up, floor by floor, until they reached their attics. At least 1,464 people drowned or died of dehydration. Entire families waited on their roofs or balconies for days, up to a week, without supplies or help. Temperatures hovered around 100 degrees. Watching the footage of the disaster, watching a catastrophe that seemed to spin on endlessly as promised rescue workers failed to materialize and dead bodies floated among the cars and rubble, I thought of Stevie Smith's famous poem: "Nobody heard him, the dead man, / But still he lay moaning: / I was much further out than you thought / And not waving but drowning. / Oh, no no no, it was too cold always / (Still the dead one lay moaning) / I was much too far out all my life / And not waving but drowning."[29]

---

26   John Biguenet, April 8, 2011.

27   Lee, Spike, director, *When the Levees Broke: A Requiem in Four Acts*, HBO, 2006. Interview with Garland Robinette, host of WWL Radio, resident of Uptown,

28   Findings of the National Oceanic and Atmospheric Administration, December 2005, reported in "More Unnatural Disasters On the Horizon" by Steven Leahy for Inter Press Service (IPS), January 11, 2006. Leahy reports: "But the most worrisome is that Katrina was not a particularly powerful storm on landfall. While it was a Category 5 strength briefly while out in the Gulf of Mexico, new data reveals that its winds were in the Category 1 or 2 class when it struck New Orleans."

29   Smith, Stevie, *Not Waving But Drowning* (London: Andre Deutsch, 1957).

Six years later, no one knows exactly how many Americans died in the aftermath of Hurricane Katrina, but, estimates run as high as 4,000 people.[30] In 2006, efforts by the state of Louisiana to deal with the missing persons and unidentified bodies abruptly ended because the project had run out of money. Today, there is "no state or federal agency that keeps track of those who remain missing from Katrina — or have since been confirmed dead. There is no central place for scattered surviving families to call."[31] Yet, although the rescue failed to arrive, the United States government managed to reopen the Port of New Orleans, a focal point for the distribution of oil and gas, within three days.[32]

"No American understands what happened here," the playwright John Biguenet told us. "They don't comprehend what it is to lose a city." When he said "American," he was not referring to himself or to the residents of New Orleans; when he said "they," he was referring to a nation outside, an almost separate country.

We were seated around a table in the library of Loyola University. The room was pale and spare, and it took on a nearly hallucinatory quality as Biguenet guided us through the modern history of New Orleans. He told us of a family, with grandparents and small children, trapped on their rooftop, in the unbearable heat, for two nights. Rescuers saw them. They came close enough to shout, "It's after 5pm and we're not authorized for overtime." Then they left. When Biguenet related this story, it was clear that the shock and pain had not left him. Immediately after the flood, New Orleans was occupied by Humvees, military and mercenaries, including Blackwater. "Everywhere you

---

30 Lindsay, Robert, "Final Katrina Death Toll at 4,081," *robertlindsay.wordpress.com* May 30, 2009 (accessed May 12, 2011). http://robertlindsay.wordpress.com/2009/05/30/final-katrina- death-toll-at-4081/

31 Olsen, Lise, "Who Died in Hurricane Katrina?" *Houston Chronicle,* August 31, 2010. www.chron.com/disp/story.mpl/nation/7177268.html

32 "Port of New Orleans Reopens After Katrina With Nine U.S. Ships," *Maritime Newspaper.* http://media.tmmarket.com:81/marex/media/newsletter/archives/old/readmorefeed.html?issue_id=120&article_id=1014&l=%3C (accessed May 12, 2011). Reporting: "The river was re-opened to commerce on Sept. 1, three days after Katrina hit, handling vessels with 12 feet of draft, such as river barges."

went," he said, "someone was holding a gun. Those guns were always cocked." Terrified of looters, the powers that be set their sights on American citizens, predominantly African-Americans. There were no helicopters because the nation's helicopters were being deployed in Iraq. In Spike Lee's documentary *When the Levees Broke,* officials describe New Orleanians who were rescued from the flooding only to be left on interstate highways "for several days, with little water, little food."[33] Desperate, some attempted to walk across the Mississippi River bridge, toward the promised buses. But, on the other side, armed men awaited them. Jefferson Parish officials had announced that they would not allow residents from Orleans Parish to cross the line. They trained their shotguns on the survivors — the elderly, the young, the injured — and ordered them to go back. Survivors had no choice but to obey.

Gina Montana, a New Orleans director, put it this way: "This was my hometown, where all of my generations, my great-great-great-grand-parents, came from. And I was so hurt and devastated to see human beings treated like cattle."[34]

In the months that followed, the suicide rate in New Orleans ballooned to twelve times the national average. Violence and desperation settled into the city. Biguenet's hands were folded tightly in front of him. "And it got worse and worse and worse."

The room was still.

He broke the silence. "Race is such a profound thread in American life."

Decades before the Civil War, de Tocqueville foresaw that race would present the greatest long-term challenge to America. Slavery would end, he knew, but its consequences might forever shackle the nation. Looking back to Europe, he observed that his countrymen had "first violated every right of humanity by their treatment of the negro and

---

33 Ray Nagin, Mayor of New Orleans, interviewed in *When the Levees Broke* (2006).
34 *Ibid.*

they afterwards informed him that these rights were precious and inviolable. They affected to open their ranks to the slaves, but the negroes who attempted to penetrate into the community were driven back with scorn; and they have incautiously and involuntarily been led to admit of freedom instead of slavery, without having the courage to be wholly iniquitous, or wholly just."[35]

In the charged decade after Lincoln's Gettysburg Address, New Orleans desegregated its public transportation system and its schools. The city's elected legislature was fifty percent black, and it succeeded in passing "the most progressive constitution the United States had ever seen." Historian Eric Foner notes that, "One hundred years before the Harlem Renaissance, Faubourg Treme was home to black poets, painters, doctors and classical composers. There was a tradition of freedom and political sophistication."

"You were born," wrote Paul Trevigne to his fellow African-Americans, as slavery came to an end, "for liberty and happiness."[36] Trevigne, a resident of New Orleans, co-founded *The Tribune,* America's first black-owned newspaper.

But, then, in 1870, Reconstruction officially ended. Federal troops withdrew from Louisiana. Month by month, year after year, the "forces of separation and apartheid began chipping away at the legal structures underpinning equality." Every single one of Louisiana's legislative gains was lost. Black students were removed, violently, from their classrooms. By 1890, twenty-five years after the end of the Civil War, "African Americans were being lynched in record numbers." In a newspaper photograph of the time, there is a close-up image of a young, murdered man, hanging from a tree, bearing the caption, "One Less Vote."[37]

Trevigne launched a final confrontation in the name of equality for all. His Citizens' Committee enlisted the cooperation of Homer Plessy

---

35 de Tocqueville, 275.
36 Newspaper articles of Paul Trevigne, *Faubourg Treme* (2008).
37 *Faubourg Treme* (2008).

who, one day in 1892, refused to move to the coloured section of the train. Plessy, who lived in Faubourg Treme, was seven-eighths white.

In his own defence, Plessy said, "I am an American citizen." He was arrested.

Plessy v. Ferguson would go all the way to the Supreme Court, which ultimately ruled against Plessy, and the idea of a truly equal African American citizenry. Immediately after the writ came down, Louisiana purged 99% of blacks from its voter rolls; New Orleans shut down all education, beyond the fifth grade, for black students. The "separate but equal" doctrine legalized discrimination, carried the full backing of the government, and would remain unchallenged until 1954. One can only imagine Trevigne's devastation, having staked so much and lost everything. "The movement failed," he wrote, "but future generations will remember."[38]

Nearly one hundred years after Plessy v. Ferguson, Dawn Logsdon and Lois Eric Lolie, both filmmakers, were in the midst of completing their documentary about the historic Faubourg Treme neighbourhood (referred to now as the 6th Ward). Aided by a 75-year-old builder named Irving Trevigne, the grandnephew of newspaperman Paul Trevigne, Lolie set about restoring his Treme home. Then, Katrina hit. The levees broke wide open. For three weeks, eighty percent of the city of New Orleans lay below water. Lolie tried to find his friends and missing family members; he and Logsdon salvaged the tapes of the documentary. Their completed work, *Faubourg Treme: The Untold Story of Black New Orleans*, released in 2008, is a devastating portrait of another America, a struggling, brave, and disturbingly invisible America.

In the last ten minutes of the film, Lolie tells us what has happened to the academics, writers, and musicians whose knowledge and remembrances are at the heart of the community: most had lost everything and could not return home. The builder, Irving Trevigne, was forced to relocate to Vermont; nine months later he passed away. Musician Glen

---

38 *Ibid.*

David Andrews told Lolie of a cherished childhood in Treme: "For me, music is the escape from the streets. Music is the college education I never got. Music is our history, it's where we come from, it's part of me."

The disaster and its aftermath had taken his house and his livelihood. "The Church where I was baptized," he said. "Gone. The cemetery with all my family. Gone.

"I don't feel like an American citizen. I know I'm not an American citizen in the eyes of the powers that be."

In Biguenet's play, *Rising Water,* a man and woman wake to find their bed surrounded by a foot of water. They climb upstairs, and then up to the attic, and finally through a vent—except that one of them, Sugar, can't get all the way through. The play ends with Camille on the roof and Sugar unable to free himself, waiting for help "that does not come." *Rising Water* has an innocence and ease that makes it all the more harrowing: how acceptable it is to be left behind. How easy it is to become detritus. Six days after the levees broke, a British news crew rescued five children who had been alone in their home for nearly a week. Having run out of necessary medication, their mother had died and now lay, in the dank humidity, on her bed. It was the first time that help had reached these children. "Here we are, day four, day five, and the Federal Government has still not made it to New Orleans," a resident said.[39]

More than forty years ago, James Baldwin wrote, "When a white man faces a black man, especially if the black man is helpless, terrible things are revealed."[40]

That Friday afternoon, we left John Biguenet and Loyola University, and stepped into the April sunshine. No one spoke much. A few hours later, our group joined the New Orleans Disaster Tour. We climbed into a shiny bus with tinted windows. Together, we passed homes that, six years later, still lay in battered ruins.

---

39 *When the Levees Broke* (2006).
40 Baldwin, "Down at the Cross," *Collected Essays,* 317.

"There's a notion of creative destruction and self-determination at the heart of one vision of America: people are infinitely capable of rising from the ashes, and are actually strengthened by it."[41] This line, penned by someone at the IWP, had been intended to help frame our journey and the lives that we would witness. But it made no sense when confronted by abandoned hospitals, boarded-up schools, and row upon row of empty lots.

"This place," the otherwise chirpy tour guide said, as we passed through a collapsed community, "is not coming back." Some black housing projects were never reopened, despite the fact that they suffered neither wind nor water damage. Some homes still bore the insignia of a spray-painted X on their walls, marking the date military units arrived at the property, the existence or non-existence of toxic water, and the number of dead animals and people.

"Imagine," the tour guide said, as we passed a trailer in front of a half disappeared house. "Still living in a trailer after all this time. Why don't these people just hurry up and fix their house?"

4

On Day Five of our Grand Tour, during a hot and sticky New Orleans afternoon, life elided into a complicated and haunting art.

We were ushered into the hushed stillness, the make-believe world, of a television set. Here, inside David Simon's HBO series, *Treme*, set three months after Hurricane Katrina, New Orleans became both real and fictional: a slender man dangled two bottles of beer by their necks; Antoine Batiste, played by actor Wendell Pierce, strode across the stage, trombone in hand. He turned to the microphone, let loose a tremor of notes. He did this over and over again, each time a little better, a little more perfectly himself.

---

41 Writers in Motion: The University of Iowa International Writing Program, http://iwp.uiowa.edu/programs/us-study-tours (link updated July 2014).

Later on, we stood with writer and director David Simon on Decatur Street, where production crew, extras, residents and tourists moved in nebulae along the pavement. He told us how life had fed his art, how he went from being a newspaperman to a dramatist, how he found a route, via fiction, to talk about what mattered to him. *Treme,* he told us, is about how New Orleans is rebuilding itself, and how culture is one of the avenues by which it is travelling back. He told us that *The Wire* and *Treme* are about ordinary people and that the stakes are human scale. "It sounds small compared to *24,*" he said, laughing. He said he wants to tell the story of what is here. He does not expect it to change anything.

Afterwards, our group retired to a nearby, cave-like, watering hole. Nataša Ďurovičová, one of our IWP hosts, made this observation: Behind the cameras on *Treme,* she said, was an all-white production team. Meanwhile African American actors, musicians, and extras were being directed like chess pieces across the set. This said something, she contended, about power structures, about who told the story, and how that story got told.

I disagreed, passionately. I questioned the simplistic lens, the ready-made window, through which she viewed these people.

Nataša acknowledged that she had never seen *Treme, The Wire,* or any of Simon's work. Regardless, she said, there was an unpleasant truth embedded in what we saw: the black actors, the white directors, the same old structures perpetuated.

Our conversation dragged on. She, a university professor, appeared comfortable in this discourse; she already knew what she was seeing long before she saw it. Yet, where she judged a white director in a white power structure, I saw artistic collaboration and a profound engagement. The argument pivoted in circles. She said that there was no denying the racial hierarchy in what we saw. I said that she gave no credit to the human beings involved. Finally, we agreed to disagree.

Later on, when this conversation was reprised with another of our hosts, he said that race, oftentimes, was easier to avoid: there were so many minefields that one could fall into, without intending to, without realizing.

But where would that leave us, I wondered. And then I wondered why we writers, from so many countries and so many histories, were here at all.

Late that night and well into the morning, Billy Kahora and I walked through the humming electricity of Frenchmen Street. We talked about *The Wire,* about this tour, about our countries and America, and then, for long, blissful moments, we just let the music cover us.

Around us, New Orleans jazz beat its pulse: now slow, now grooving, now heady. *Treme* was filming a sidewalk scene: authentic drinkers (with real drinks) and film set drinkers (with fake drinks) blurred together, and I watched in tipsy fascination as life merged with a rewritten, structured, refolded, life.

Billy told me that, in a few weeks, he would deliver a talk in Philadelphia that the University organizers had titled, "Why I Live in Kenya." He shook his head and we both burst out laughing. I tried to imagine Philip Roth or Annie Proulx arriving in Nairobi, tasked with holding forth on the subject of, "Why I Live in America." Years of writing and thought and observation would be sheared away, so that the writer could fit through the narrowest of keyholes.

"It is as though," wrote Ralph Ellison, "I have been surrounded by mirrors of hard, distorting glass. When they approach me they see only my surroundings, themselves, or figments of their imagination — indeed, everything and anything except me."[42] "This had nothing," as Baldwin wrote, "to do with anything I was, or contained, or could become."[43]

I told Billy that I had not expected race to be such a defining theme of our journey. Billy admitted to being less surprised. He recalled how Charlie had told us that cities where race was, and is, an issue had

---

42 Ellison, Ralph, *Invisible Man* (New York: Vintage, 1983).
43 Baldwin, "Down at the Cross," *Collected Essays,* 307.

suffered the most catastrophic declines: Detroit, Cleveland, St. Louis, Baltimore. In the economic downturn, some cities, unable to sustain themselves, might wither away. Officials in Flint, Michigan, for instance, believe that their city will have to contract by at least forty percent in order to survive, moving residents and services into a smaller area and abandoning the rest to nature.[44] Is there, in the future, a smaller, leaner America?

My thoughts were uneasy. The terms on which we had been brought here — to read the fall and write the recovery — no longer felt adequate; they seemed like land already cleared, already developed, a cut and paste template of America. I felt myself drawn down another path entirely, away from our hosts, away from Nataša, towards a way of looking that seemed, as yet, untidy and unclear.

Billy motioned to the bartender for another drink. A man slapped his guitar, bowed his head, and played a jangling riff.

I told Billy that I was reading the *Collected Essays of James Baldwin*.

He smiled broadly. "It will change your life."

The Grand Tour hurtled on. After long days in the field, we were summoned to meetings to ensure we had done the required readings. Awkward conversations ensued on American exceptionalism and American optimism. The rift between our hosts and me deepened. "Poor stumblers," Ellison once wrote, "neither of you can see the other."[45] I found myself constantly biting my tongue. I was trying, and failing, to understand why I was here, and what, if anything, the IWP and the State Department expected. In fourteen days, what could I see of America that would be more than a blurred distortion? Would our journey become the intellectual equivalent of Nataša's five-minute glimpse through the keyhole, into the set of *Treme*?

---

44 Leonard, Tom, "U.S. Cities May Have to Be Bulldozed to Survive," *The Telegraph*, June 12, 2009.
45 Ellison, Ralph, *Invisible Man* (New York: Vintage, 1995).

A scheduled visit to a Lafayette church ended in confusion and misunderstanding. Our group had been brought here, Nataša said, to see volunteerism, a defining characteristic of American life. On a half-moon stage at Trinity Bible Church, the Pastor retold the story of God's parting of the Red Sea.

"The country you are about to conquer: Syria, Iraq, Palestine, Egypt, Jordan, Lebanon, they're not going to just pack up their homes and go. There's going to be a war." His face radiated sunshine. The congregation, well-dressed and well-heeled, wore unreadable expressions. The pastor asked us to celebrate the blessings of God's constancy and the enduring promise of the Holy Land. "God never reneges on a promise. It's not about how good Moses is. It's about the goodness of God. *I will give you every place where you set your foot.* God promised the land."

After 45 minutes, I stood up and quietly left; I was not the only one to do so.

During the service, Ed fell into conversation with a friendly church volunteer. He told her we had just come from New Orleans. Thinking of the incompetency of FEMA and the federal government, he asked her how this catastrophe could have befallen the residents of New Orleans.

Without doubt, without hesitation, she told him, "It happens to people who put their faith in institutions other than God."

Another volunteer told us, "Some people just seem incapable of helping themselves."

Outside, the church's blinking signboard gleamed against the highway. Find us on Facebook, it said. And then it blinked and slowly faded out.

"If you were lucky in the world," wrote Frederick Barthelme, in his post-Katrina novel, *Waveland*, "you built yourself a new life as an adult, complete with friends, lovers, partners, rivals, enemies. You replaced the old people with new people, and your party moved along effortlessly, dancing toward death. If you were unlucky you were left to float on the great angry ocean, never to hear the sound of wood hitting wood in the middle of the night in the darkness of the sea."

Three days later, we met, by chance, T.R. German, Jr.

"Where you all from?" he asked, in mock surprise. We tried to explain that we were a Cambodian from Australia, a Malaysian-Chinese from Canada, a Burmese living in Pittsburgh, a Scotland-based Jamaican, a Kenyan, a Filipino, a Bosnian, and an Iranian-American. T.R. smiled. A grizzled, jovial man, he happened to be volunteering that morning at the 16th Street Baptist Church in Birmingham, Alabama.

In the 1960s, this church had been the focal point of a Birmingham community ready to take, through peaceful civil disobedience, civil rights long denied. Then, on a Sunday morning in September 1963, four men, members of the Ku Klux Klan, colluded in planting 19 sticks of dynamite outside the church's stairwell. One of the bombers, Robert Chambliss, boasted that, by the time he was through, "They will be begging for segregation." The dynamite exploded just after ten in the morning, injuring 22 people and killing four young schoolgirls.

We sat in the first two pews, trying to take in the history of this place, this city. I thought of a young man I had met the day before, just around the corner from here. He had been sitting on a plastic chair in front of a barber shop. We had talked about Birmingham, the strange stillness of its downtown core. He was curious about Canada, and when I invited him to email me, he paused and looked concerned. "I haven't got any email just now," he said. And then, a few minutes later, he asked me, "With email, how does that work exactly? You just send it on a computer?" I was taken aback. He was about 18 years old but, in the richest country in the world, he had not yet had the opportunity to explore the internet, to send an email. I told him to go to Yahoo or Gmail, that it would be easy to sign up, that he only needed to type his message and hit send. I wrote down my email address. He wished me the best of luck, the safest of travels. "Some day," he said, "you'll hear from me."

"This is not a museum," T.R. said, "We are a church that is alive." He told us that he believed that these four little girls had been protected by God in some way; their bodies, he said, were "not dismantled."

Patiently, for nearly an hour, T.R. took our questions and then lobbed them gently aside. When we pressed him on race, on history, he said, "Who's crazy? Something's not right with them all." He told us to keep a wide berth from ignorance, and to remember we had been blessed by God. He said, "In the United States, the most segregated day of the week is Sunday, when everyone goes off to their different churches." "We got a black president," he said, "and he can't do nothing. What's wrong? I don't understand. I don't understand." Quietly, almost against his will, he said, "The system has not changed. It's a touchy thing. But it's alright." And finally he said that, if we chose to write about the four girls who died here, we should use their names, Addie Mae Collins, Carole Robertson, Cynthia Wesley, and Denise McNair. "Everyone has a name," he said. Once more, he told us, "I don't understand."

"There should be a song, /" wrote my fellow writer Kei Miller, "for the man whose life has not been the stuff of ballads, / but has lived each day in incredible and untrumpeted ways."[46]

In this country, African Americans were once defined by the Constitution as "three-fifths" of a man.[47] "There's no way in the world you can even imagine what it was like," Irving Trevigne, the house builder, said when questioned about the years of segregation. He had appeared pained and vulnerable. "What could you do? There was nothing you could do. All the laws were against you... It's hard to imagine if you didn't live it."[48] The laws have changed, but the attitudes, as de Tocqueville presciently noted, would prove to be more intransigent: "Slavery recedes, but the prejudice to which it has given birth remains stationary." Five years ago, 35,000 people were abandoned in the Superdome of

46 Miller, Kei, "Unsung," *A Light Song of Light* (Manchester: Carcanet, 2010) 42.

47 Baldwin, "Down at the Cross," *Collected Essays,* 335.

48 *Faubourg Treme* (2008).

New Orleans without adequate water, food, or medical supplies. Conditions were too dangerous, authorities claimed, for them to get inside. It was a white woman who cried out, from the mass of humanity in the stadium, "This is not about low income. It's not about rich people, poor people. It's about people."[49] On their faces, black and white, I could see anger, grief, and shock.

On the faces of the old, I saw resignation.

Trevigne, exiled to Vermont before his death, must have wondered if the deep roots of his family had finally been pulled loose, if his great-uncle's words could carry them any further: "The movement failed, but future generations will remember."

"It is entirely unacceptable," wrote James Baldwin, "that I should have no voice in the political affairs of my own country, for I am not a ward of America; I am one of the first Americans to arrive on these shores."[50]

Our very last stop was Birmingham's Civil Rights Institute. On that morning, we were given the choice of skipping this visit entirely. It was one of the only times we had been given such an option and some in our group, myself included, objected. However, the rigours of modern travel (a plane to catch) meant that we were rushed, in fifty minutes, through its displays. Here, finally, was part of the history and context I had been waiting for. How, I had wondered, did a country go from the Civil War and Lincoln's Gettysburg Address to the derelict poverty of West Baltimore? How did America move from Jim Crow to the catastrophic flooding of New Orleans? Did anyone—historians, curators, teachers—know the answers? The story at the centre, the Civil Rights Movement, which shook and inspired people in my country and so many others, had boiled over here in Birmingham. "One day," Martin Luther King had said, writing from his Birmingham prison cell, "the South will recognize its real heroes... One day the South will know

49   *When the Levees Broke* (2006).
50   Baldwin, "Down at the Cross," *Collected Essays,* 718.

that when these disinherited children of God sat down at lunch counters, they were in reality standing up for what is best in the American
dream."[51] I saw Khet reading from the placards, utterly motionless, lost
in thought. I saw another history spanning powerfully into her own. I
thought of the words of Cambodia's Prime Minister, Hun Sen, in response to the ongoing investigation into the Khmer Rouge regime:
"We should dig a hole and bury the past and look ahead to the 21th
century with a clean slate."

The fifty minutes we had at the Civil Rights Institute, this precious
place, evaporated. Our host came to gather us up. I was still standing
in 1963. When I came outside, into the deserted downtown core of
the city, into the sunshine and closed-up shopfronts, the poverty,
and the relics of neon signs, I did not know where I stood.

"Time's up," our host said, apologetically, kindly. "History ends here."

5

Over the course of nearly two weeks, our group of writers spoke to
more than a dozen people — historians, city planners, curators, writers,
professors, hunters and fishers, oil rig workers — but, for reasons that
are still not clear to me, we never heard an African American voice (or
indeed, any minority voice, including Native American). Even in our
last stop, Birmingham, a city that is nearly 75% African American,[52]
both of our guides were white (including historian Pamela King, who
was the only woman). T.R. German was unplanned; a chance meeting,
a lucky accident.

At first, I thought it was a case of best intentions: perhaps, when
seeking out candidates, a person's race had simply never come into
play. Later on, when I asked one of our hosts why no black guides or

---

51   King, Martin Luther, "Letter from a Birmingham Jail," http://www.uiowa.edu/giwp/texts/MLK-
birminhamJail.html (accessed May 7, 2011).

52   Wikipedia contributors, "Birmingham, Alabama," *Wikipedia, The Free Encyclopedia,* http://en.
wikipedia.org/wiki/Birmingham,_Alabama (accessed April 30, 2011).

scholars had been included, he said, confused and taken aback, "There were none."

It was Day 13. In Washington, DC, in front of State Department officials, I pointed out how discomforting it was, how unexpected, that each and every one of our drivers—in every taxi, shuttlebus, tour bus and transit van—had been black. I said that I found it inexplicable that no black historians, artists, writers, or thinkers had been a part of our itinerary. Afterwards, one of our hosts took me aside and said he felt we needed to speak about the issues I had regarding race. I had no issues, I said, only questions. We had been moved and troubled by what we saw: what had they expected? Did they not feel the same? The conversation ended in awkward silence. Late that night, one of the other writers said to me, "If you were black, you wouldn't be encountering this kind of resistance to your criticisms." I thought it was even more tragic than that. Within two weeks, we had fallen into the scenario that Charlie had described in Baltimore: we saw the same things, lived the same days, but there was a firebreak—a shortage of words, a turning away—between us.

The day before we came home, one of our hosts sat us down and reiterated the importance of the long essay we were expected to submit. We must put our best foot forward, she said, because these essays would be read by important people in the State Department, the "bigwigs."

I asked if this fact should change the nature of what I chose to write about.

Of course not, she said.

I wondered if it would change the quality of what I wrote. She did not answer.

I knew I was being wilfully blind, that I was an irritant; the program needed to maintain State Department funding and support. But that was their bureaucratic discourse, not mine, not ours. We had been invited as writers, as thinkers, as equals.

It was our last night. We were invited to the home of friends of the State Department. Nataša accompanied us—the four writers who had agreed to go—and we arrived at a gracious and elegant home filled with the carvings, rugs, and porcelain dishes our hosts—professors and government consultants—had accumulated in Africa and Asia. They did not put out enough chairs for their five guests. I sat on the floor and listened as our hosts went on about themselves and their visits to Africa. I ate all the cheese and thought of the sharp and courageous words my fellow writers had written, not only these last two weeks, but in the many years preceding. I thought of Khet's brave criticisms of the Burmese government, of her imprisonment. I thought of Adisa's cutting stories of the war in Bosnia, of Alice's memoir, *Unpolished Gem*, published when she was still in her twenties, and the profound humour and insight with which she writes about her Cambodian-Chinese-Australian childhood. Reading her work, I had recognized my own immigrant parents, their aspirations and hopes, their devastations, "the semi-dazed dream they entered when they rested from too many taxi-shifts, or when they closed their eyes from the fatigue of opening too many stitched buttonholes. They realized their children were watchers just as they were." She wrote about ways in which words themselves seemed to disappear: "What were important were the big questions, the big questions we never asked each other, for lack of words."[53]

I looked around at the salon in which we sat, the exotic objects that gleamed with haunting beauty. Our hosts' monologue continued, and I wondered, not for the first time, why we were here and when we might leave.

Weeks later, when I returned home, a friend of mine said to me, "Yours is a journey so many Americans dream of taking, but the opportunity never comes." She had grown up in New York during the Civil Rights Movement; how I wished that she, that someone with her sensitivities, had accompanied us. Her questions, her doubt, her desire to

---

53   Pung, Alice, *Unpolished Gem: My Mother, My Grandmother, and Me* (New York: Plume, 2009) 186, 150.

see how the story came together, would have informed and enlightened me. Jason England, an assistant at the IWP, had put together our reading list: in these texts, one could see a vision for what this tour might have been, and a deep engagement with the challenges at the heart of our journey. In January of this year, he wrote to us, "It's impossible to quantify my enthusiasm about this program's potential to be historically edifying and philosophically challenging... One might expect the information to inspire some righteous indignation, as well as sadness and frustration." He welcomed the idea that history and knowledge might lead to a greater incoherence, that there was no easy salve, no blind and simple judgement.

Due to illness, he was forced to withdraw from our trip. Our hosts rarely mentioned him.

The road that I wanted to cut for myself still lay in brambles. The more I tried to see, the more the country seemed to grow chaotic, slippery, distant. "I, too," said Ellison, "have become acquainted with ambivalence."[54]

"I am an invisible man," he famously wrote. "I am a man of substance, of flesh and bone, fibre and liquids—and I might even be said to possess a mind. I am invisible, understand, simply because people refuse to see me."[55]

"Invisibility," the radio broadcaster Terry O'Reilly said, "oppresses by omission."[56]

Every 45 minutes, a football field's worth of land disappears in southern Louisiana, lost to coastal erosion.[57] The very shape of America is

---

54 Ellison, 10.
55 Ellison, 3.
56 O'Reilly, Terry, "Diversity in Advertising," *The Age of Persuasion*. CBC Radio. Broadcast date June 18, 2011.
57 "The Rise and Disappearance of Southeast Louisiana," http://www.nola.com/speced/lastchance/multimedia/flash.ssf?flashlandloss1.swf (accessed April 24, 2011).

changing, literally, minute by minute. Near the end of our Grand Tour, we stood on solid ground that, for our children's generation, will be lost underwater. We had the privilege to think about the change that is coming, that is here, what Billy Kahora described as "slow death by a thousand economic cuts." Our parents and grandparents' generation may have known something of this loss, having lived the 20th century in places from Malaysia to Burma to Cambodia, Bosnia, and Iran: they carried unspoken stories, abandoned neighbourhoods, lives and countries lost to war, conflict, emigration, economic collapse, nature.

Two months have passed since I returned home, and I know that something of my ability to comprehend America has been broken. Despite having lived across the border nearly all my life, I had not anticipated race to be the defining framework of our travels; in my ignorance, I had not realized how long the road is, and that the great historical disaster of slavery, the failure of Reconstruction to preserve movements toward equality, the generations pinned down by Jim Crow laws, the division enshrined in schools, the disaster of urban planning that demolished neighbourhoods, that favoured one community over another, the blight that stalked the inner cities, the violence, drugs, and degradation of poverty, the snakelike twisting of the law to keep one group in their place: all these are part of the same decline. I do not know how to write about the recovery because I do not know where it begins. Perhaps it is not prosperity that leads to renewal, but something more painful, something akin to the loss of myths that were never, finally, true: that progress will continue, that America is exceptional, that democracy had been attained. "I know what I am asking is impossible,"[58] Baldwin wrote in 1962, and yet he held out hope that America was on the brink of changing, if only the moment was seized.

Twenty-four years later, that hope was gone. "When I was young," he wrote, "I was being told it will take time before a Black person can be treated as a human being here, but it will happen. We will help to

---

58 Baldwin, "Down at the Cross," *Collected Essays,* 346.

make it happen. We promise you... No promise was kept with them, no promise was kept with me, nor can I counsel those coming after me to believe a word uttered by my morally bankrupt and desperately dishonest countrymen."[59]

Baldwin died in 1987, and did not live to see the catastrophe of New Orleans.

I know that the transition in America mirrors what is happening in my own country, that many of our blind spots and disgraces are the same,[60] that people of all nations and all creeds forget, that if we may choose what to believe, we must seek wisely, counselled by knowledge and by history, and not by ignorance, not by a belief in an exceptional people or a manifest destiny, but in acknowledgment of what Martin Luther King, Jr. called, "an inescapable network of mutuality, tied in a single garment of destiny."[61]

On the way to DC, our flight was delayed in Memphis. I had a chance to scrutinize the images of terrorists framed and mounted by the

---

59 Baldwin, "Introduction to Notes of a Native Son," *Collected Essays*, 813.

60 "Approximately three thousand Black Loyalists sailed to Nova Scotia between April and November of 1783, travelling on both Navy vessels and British chartered private transports." Racism in Canada was nothing short of rampant and horrifying. "In 1782, the first race riot in North America took place in Birchtown, with white soldiers attacking the black settlers who were getting work that the soldiers thought they should have. Due to the unkept promises of the British government and the discrimination from the white colonists, 1,192 African American men, women and children left Nova Scotia on January 15, 1792 and established Freetown, Sierra Leone." Quoted material from Wikipedia contributors, "Black Nova Scotians," Wikipedia, The Free Encyclopedia, http://en.wikipedia.org/wiki/Black_Nova_Scotians (accessed May 31, 2011). Those who stayed, and who continued arriving, hoping to escape discrimination in America, lived in separate all-black villages and towns. In the 1960s, the Canadian governments, federal and provincial, worked to demolish these historic towns. The town of Africville was infamously emptied between 1964 and 1967, and all its residents relocated. "The residents were assisted in their move by Halifax literally moving the Africvillians with the city dump trucks... Only 14 residents held clear legal titles to their land. Those with no legal rights were given a $500 payment and promised a furniture allowance, social assistance, and public housing units." Quoted material from Wikipedia contributors, "Africville," Wikipedia, The Free Encyclopedia, http://en.wikipedia.org/wiki/Africville (accessed May 31, 2011). Further information on Africville can be found at www.africville.ca Canada's relationship with race and with its First Nations peoples is a large, unhappy, and difficult topic, one that demands a discussion all its own.

61 King, "Letter from a Birmingham Jail" (1963).

Department of Homeland Security. Several weeks later, on May 2nd, I attended a reception at the home of the American Ambassador in Ottawa, Canada. The night before I had stayed up with other writers and watched, in stunned silence, the rolling coverage of the assassination of Osama bin Laden: thousands of Americans crowded into the streets, celebrating victory. The next morning, a diplomat spoke briefly about how proud she was, on this day, to be an American. I thought about all I had seen. I thought about New Orleans and Baltimore, and I wondered what event might take place, what acknowledgement, that would allow America's diplomats to make this same avowal of pride in a foreign country. What would need to happen, remembering the 4,000 dead and missing of New Orleans, in order to feel that justice was served? If we can answer this question, perhaps the recovery may yet begin. But the question itself does not seem to exist.

James Baldwin has my guiding light these last few months, and I think he deserves to lay claim to the title of visionary and great American writer. He saw the downhill slide and his essays were, decades ago, warnings for what might be, warnings of a lack of justice that had taken root in his country. We must become human or irrelevant, he believed. "Now, this country is going to be transformed. It will not be transformed by an act of God, but by all of us, by you and me. I don't believe any longer that we can afford to say that it is entirely out of our hands."[62]

---

62 Baldwin, "Notes for a Hypothetical Novel," *Collected Essays*, 230.

Reading List

James Baldwin, "Notes for a Hypothetical Novel," in *James Baldwin: Collected Essays* (Library of America, 2008)

John Biguenet, *Rising Water* and *Shotgun* (plays, 2006 and 2009); "New Orleans: Where the Future Arrives First" (no date)

David Blight, *Frederick Douglass and Abraham Lincoln: A Relationship in Language, Politics, and Memory* (Marquette University Press, 2001)

Frederick Douglass, "'What, to the American slave, is your 4th of July?' The Independence Day Speech" (1852)

Barbara Ehrenreich, *Bright-Sided: How Positive Thinking Is Undermining America* (Henry Holt, 2010)

Kent Gramm, *November: Lincoln's Elegy at Gettysburg* (Indiana University Press, 2001)

John Jakle and David Wilson, *Derelict Landscapes: The Wasting of America's Built Environment* (Rowman & Littlefield, 1992)

Dr. Martin Luther King, Jr., "Letter from Birmingham Jail" (1963)

Abraham Lincoln, "The Gettysburg Address" (1863)

John McPhee, *The Control of Nature* (G.K. Hall, 1999)

Peter Schuck and James Wilson, eds.: *Understanding America: The Anatomy of an Exceptional Nation* (Public Affairs Books, 2008)

Rebecca Solnit, *A Paradise Built in Hell: The Extraordinary Communities That Arise in Disaster* (Viking, 2009)

Sharon Zukin, *Naked City: the Death and Life of Authentic Urban Places* (Oxford University Press, 2008)

Contributors

ADISA BAŠIĆ, born in 1979, studied Comparative Literature, German and Librarianship at the University of Sarajevo, earned an M.A. in Human Rights and Democracy, and published a first poetry collection at the age of nineteen. Her second poetry volume, *Trauma-Market,* appeared in 2004 and the award-winning collection "A Promo Clip for my Homeland" in 2010. She has participated in many regional and European poetry events, and is widely published in regional literary magazines. She writes on cultural affairs for the independent weekly *Slobodna Bosna*.

VICENTE GARCIA GROYON won the Manila Critics Circle National Book Award both for the novel *The Sky Over Dimas* (2004) and for *On Cursed Ground and Other Stories* (2005); he is the editor of several anthologies and collections of Filipino fiction. He has written four film scripts, including *Agaton and Mindy* (2009) and *Namets!* (2008), and directed several shorts. He teaches creative writing at De La Salle University in Manila.

EDUARDO HALFÓN, born in Guatemala City in 1971, has an engineering degree from North Carolina State University. His novels include *Esto no es una pipa, Saturno, De cabo roto, El ángel literario, El boxeador polaco,* and *La pirueta,* which won the José María de Pereda Prize for Short Novel in Santander, Spain. His short fiction has been published in English, French, Italian, Portuguese, Serbian, and Dutch. He has taught literature at Guatemala's Universidad Francisco Marroquín; in 2007 the Bogotá Hay Festival listed him as one of "39 best young Latin American writers."

BILLY KARANJA KAHORA is the managing editor of the Kenya-based journal *Kwani?* and of the Picha Mtaani/Kwani book project, and has edited the collection *Kenya Burning.* His writings have been published in *Granta, Kwani?* and *Vanity Fair;* he has a book of creative nonfiction, *The True Story of David Munyakei* (2009), and script credits for *Soul Boy* (2010), and *Nairobi Half-Life* (2011).

KHET MAR is a journalist, novelist, short story writer, poet and essayist born in Burma. Author of the novel *Wild Snowy Night,* three collections of short stories and a volume of essays, she has had work translated into Japanese, Spanish and English, broadcast, and made into a film. In 2009 she was a featured writer at the PEN Word Voices Festival, and subsequently writer-in-residence at City of Asylum/Pittsburgh, which provides sanctuary to writers exiled under threat of severe persecution in their native countries.

KEI MILLER is the author of three books of poetry, two novels and a collection of short stories, and the editor of the anthology *New Caribbean Poetry* (Carcanet, 2007). Short-listed for a number of major literary awards, he is the recipient of Jamaica's Silver Musgrave medal and the Una Marson Prize for Literature. He teaches creative writing at the University of Glasgow.

ALICE PUNG was born in Melbourne to Cambodian parents. Her memoir *Unpolished Gem* won the 2006 Australian Book Industry Association award for Newcomer of the Year, and other prizes. Her work was included in *Best Australian Short Stories 2007.* A story collection, *Growing Up Asian in Australia,* appeared in 2008; a second memoir, *Her Father's Daughter,* appeared in 2011. A lawyer by trade, she contributes regularly to *The Monthly* and *The Age.*

MADELEINE THIEN is the author of *Simple Recipes,* a collection of stories, and *Certainty,* a novel, which was a finalist for the Kiriyama Prize and won the Amazon.ca/Books in Canada First Novel Award. Her work has appeared in *Granta, The Walrus, Five Dials, Brick,* and the *Asia Literary Review,* and been translated into sixteen languages. In 2010 she received the Ovid Festival Prize, awarded to an international writer of promise. Her novel *Dogs at the Perimeter* came out in 2011.

EDITORS

NATAŠA ĎUROVIČOVÁ is the house editor of the International Writing Program at the University of Iowa, where she also teaches courses on aspects of translation, international literature, and cinema. Her academic publications mainly concern translation in the history of cinema.

HUGH FERRER is the associate director of the International Writing Program and a senior editor at the *Iowa Review*. He teaches at the Iowa Summer Writing Festival and serves as a board member at the University of Iowa Center for Human Rights and the Iowa City UNESCO City of Literature.

Three hundred fifty copies of *Fall and Rise, American Style* were printed & bound at Thomson-Shore printers in Dexter, Michigan. The essays are composed in Sumner Stone's Magma type and the titling appears in Parisine Plus, designed by Jean François Porchez. 91st Meridian Books recognizes in its editing policies that literary English comes in a range of regional varieties.

FIRST EDITION